THE YORKSHIRE RIPPER

A Star Original

'No one can ever know what it is like when your child is murdered. I wept when I heard about Josephine Whitaker. For those they left behind there will never be peace again . . . A murder doesn't just end with the victim. It spreads hideous ripples throughout a family. In a way it kills them all.'

THE
YORKSHIRE RIPPER

Michael Nicholson

A STAR BOOK

published by
the Paperback Division of
W. H. ALLEN & Co. Ltd.

A Star Book
Published in 1979
by the Paperback Division of
W. H. Allen & Co. Ltd
A Howard and Wyndham Company
44 Hill Street, London W1X 8LB

Copyright © Michael Nicholson, 1979

Printed in Great Britain by
Hunt Barnard Printing Ltd, Aylesbury, Bucks.

ISBN 0 352 30616 5

Contents

THE YORKSHIRE RIPPER

Acknowledgments

My grateful thanks to my wife Noreen who has undertaken the transcription of a large amount of barely legible longhand much of it harrowing in content.

I am similarly grateful to Rene Cutforth whose foreword bestows a little distinction on this volume.

I'm also indebted to David Cowell, Lecturer in Criminology at the Polytechnic of Central London for guiding me through the academic minefield of psychopathy and related disorders. My thanks also to my old friend and colleague Jonathan Avory who has given me such valuable advice and who has contributed significantly to this book. I am sincerely grateful to Professor Terence Morris of the LSE for his friendly interest and for pointing me in the direction of profitable avenues of research. Finally, I would like to thank Michael Fowell who gave me such valuable assistance with the more hazardous aspects of my research.

My thanks to the numerous friendly people in Yorkshire, Lancashire and Manchester who have taken the time to sup a glass with me and discuss the murderous exploits of the Ripper.

The kind assistance of the cuttings library of the newspapers listed below has been of inestimable value. Photographs derived from these sources are acknowledged separately.

My thanks to: *The Yorkshire Evening Post*
Telegraph and Argus, Bradford
Manchester Evening News
Lancashire Evening Post
Huddersfield Examiner
London Evening Standard

WEST YORKSHIRE METROPOLITAN POLICE
Chief Constable: Ronald Gregory Esq. QPM DL
Criminal Investigation Department
Assistant Chief Constable: G. A. Oldfield Esq. QPM
Area Headquarters, Leeds
Detective Chief Superintendent: Denis Hoban (died 15th March 1978)
CID
Detective Chief Superintendent J. Hobson (Deputy to ACC Crime)
Area Headquarters, Bradford
CID: Detective Chief Superintendent G. T. Lapish
Detective Superintendent D. Holland (Head of Ripper Squad)
Detective Chief Superintendent Peter Gilrain

GREATER MANCHESTER POLICE
Chief Constable: C. J. Anderton Esq. QPM FBIM
Crime
Central Crime Area: Chief Superintendent J. Ridgway Esq.

LANCASHIRE CONSTABULARY
Chief Constable: A. Laugharne Esq. QPM
Deputy Chief Constable: J. W. Moody Esq. OBE QPM
Criminal Investigation
Detective Chief Superintendent W. Brooks Esq.

NORTHUMBRIA POLICE
Chief Constable: S. E. Bailey Esq. QPM
Deputy Chief Constable: W. Baharie Esq. OBE QPM
Assistant Chief Constable (Crime): R. B. Johnson Esq.

CLEVELAND CONSTABULARY
Chief Constable: C. F. Payne Esq. QPM
Deputy Chief Constable: W. G. Ashton Esq. MBE MBIM
Assistant Chief Constable (Operations): H. R. Hill Esq.
HQ 'C' Division, CID: Detective Chief Superintendent N. Hudson Esq.

Foreword

The murderer known as the 'Yorkshire Ripper' has so far claimed twelve victims since 1975, all of them horribly mutilated, most, but not all, of them prostitutes or what the police call 'good time girls' : four other women have escaped him with their lives, but at the cost of terrible injuries, and twenty-three children have been orphaned. Police investigations up to date have concentrated the energies of vast numbers of policemen and cost several millions of pounds, all, apparently, to no avail.

M. J. Nicholson, the author of this book, ends it with these words : 'If he has not been brought to book, I hope that some of the ideas contained here may provoke a thought or a recollection which will lead to the murderer.' To that end he has collected, not, of course, everything that is known about the murders, because the police have decided not to release some of their information, but everything that can be got at. That, on the surface, seems quite a bit, since it includes a tape recording of the killer's voice, letters in his handwriting and descriptions of him by women who just escaped death at his hands. Nevertheless he is still at large and growing more reckless. Recent victims have not been prostitutes, *ipso facto* vulnerable to attack, but perfectly ordinary teenage girls. Large rewards have been offered, hundreds of police have spent over a quarter of a million man-hours interviewing many thousands of people, over 20,000 statements have been taken. Miracles of police investigative work have been accomplished – of four hundred people who casually happened to be in a certain street on the night of one of the murders, the police managed to trace three hundred and eighty. All the best professional advice has been sought and every technical forensic aid has been employed. The personal commitment of the officers leading the investigation has been total : but the file is still open.

In his research for this book Michael Nicholson has interviewed hundreds of people concerned, however peripherally, with the case, digested innumerable newspaper files and visited the six Northern towns where the attacks have occurred. His account of this terrible subject is cool, clear and detached. He considers the formidable practical problems that the murderer has so far overcome, the absence of fingerprints, the disposal and replacement of blood-stained clothing, the concealment of the weapon, the evasion of police patrols and car checks, and, above all, the avoidance of witnesses. But besides giving a detailed, and, as far as is possible, an unsensational account of the circumstances and background of each of the crimes, he widens the subject to consider the psychopathology of the multiple killer. Peter Kurten, the Dusseldorf killer of the 1920s, Dr Petiot during the German occupation of Paris, Christie and the West London Stripper and others are considered to find any lessons that can be drawn by those who are on the trail of the Yorkshire murderer. Above all, any analogies with the Jack the Ripper murders in Victorian Whitechapel may be important, because the man responsible for the Northern murders signs himself boastfully 'Jack the Ripper' in two letters to Assistant Chief Constable George Oldfield, and refers to himself as Jack in the tape recording which has been the centre of so much investigation.

In this recording, the Ripper says, of prostitutes : 'They never learn, do they, George? I bet you've warned them, but they never listen.' This point, the extraordinary passive and accepting attitude of many of the girls and women who may reasonably expect to meet the Ripper in one of the run-down red light areas of an inner city slum, or kerb-crawling along a motorway link road, is one of the most bizarre and disturbing aspects of the whole case, and Michael Nicholson has a good deal to say upon the subject of prostitution and the way of life of the prostitute that, although uncomfortable reading, strikes me as just and accurate.

To my mind, much of the value of this book lies in the powerful indictment the author makes of those planning experts, who, from the highest motives, no doubt, have afflicted many of our great cities, including the six with which he concerns himself here, with acres of derelict waste ground and scabrous tower blocks, providing the criminal with a happy hunting ground and simplifying his get-away by quick and easy links to the motorways. 'It could be argued that the Ripper is one of the few beneficiaries of the planning process,' he says. For that one sentence alone I would applaud this book, but there are others, many ...

RENÉ CUTFORTH

Introduction

*'And Cain said to Abel his brother: "Let us go forth abroad."
And when they were in a field, Cain rose up against his
brother Abel and slew him.*

*'And the Lord said to Cain: "Where is thy brother Abel?"
And he answered: "I know not. Am I my brother's keeper?"*

*'And He said to him: "What has thou done? The voice of
thy brother's blood crieth to me from the earth. Now, therefore, cursed shalt thou be upon the earth." '*

In all civilised societies the crime of murder is the most
disturbing and distressing of all transgressions of the human
and moral law. The more civilised the society the greater
premium that is put on the value of individual life. The
murderer therefore attacks the whole structure of human
social values. The act of murder is final and irreversible, it is
a negation of our profoundest instincts which are to nourish,
maintain and extend our lives. Small wonder therefore
that the murderer is so often driven to take his own life in
remorse, expiation for his crime or as a result of his own
madness. Most murders are, in the language of a Leeds crime
reporter, 'fish and chip' affairs, domestic or social incidents
where murderer and victim are related or at least
acquainted. On the night of the Ripper's first murder, for
example a woman strangled a man to death in a telephone
box. The bizarre incident rated no more than a brief mention
in the *Yorkshire Evening Post* and the subsequent arrest
justified a mere couple of lines of reporting.

Only a mercifully very small proportion of murderers

commit more than one murder and the phenomenon of the mass killer is extremely rare. In most cases the killer and the victim are closely acquainted and in many instances the crime is, in police parlance, 'self-detecting'.

The presence of a mass sadistic killer in the cities of West Yorkshire and beyond has, in contrast to the conventional pattern of murder, had a chilling and horrifying impact. To date he has claimed no less than twelve victims, more than any murderer in Britain in this century. In all cases the victims were women, and again in all cases their bodies had been subject to the most horrible mutilations. So long as he remains undetected fear will stalk the Pennine towns.

George Oldfield, Head of West Yorkshire CID and Assistant Chief Constable, was in overall charge of the multi-million pound investigations from early on. Public interest has been enormous, journalistic pressure immense. Enquiries have poured in from all over the world and Mr Oldfield has been woken in the small hours by radio broadcasters telephoning from as far away as Australia, whilst Los Angeles reporters have descended fresh from their investigations of the Hollywood Strangler. There is even a film being shot in Leeds Chapeltown, where the Ripper has struck four times. This has drawn criticism from Mr George Oldfield who described it as in bad taste; and also from the local prostitute community. One woman was quoted as saying, 'The parents and relatives of the Ripper victims have suffered enough without having a film draw attention to what has happened.'

Early in the football season, in August 1979, the BBC televised a League match between Sunderland and Fulham. Beneath the commentary a persistent chant was audible: 'There's only one Jack the Ripper.' This mindless slogan to the tune of 'Guantanamera' was taken up by a significant proportion of Sunderland supporters. This rather tended to support the notion that we were witnessing the genesis of another Ripper legend: the Ripper, whether we like it or not, seems well on the way to becoming a folk hero lionised for his audacity, though not of course for his murderous acts.

One intriguing aspect of this case is the extent to which the mass killer has modelled himself on Jack the Ripper. Whether the Victorian slayer inspired him to kill is doubtful. It is more likely that the enormous press interest has created an image in the killer's mind which he has subsequently reinforced by his own imitative behaviour. He is, as it were, playing up to the audience. The most obvious similarity is the murders themselves, which exhibit the same kinds of savagery and mutilation. Secondly, the lifestyle of many of the victims is similar. There is evidence that, as in the case of Jack, many of the victims had been drinking and were in certain cases intoxicated. They were therefore at their most defenceless and unsuspecting, and it seems likely that the killer observed their condition whilst formulating his plan to murder. The crimes of this latterday Ripper have been mainly perpetrated in the inner city slums, the nearest contemporary conditions approaching those prevailing in nineteeenth-century Whitechapel.

The first chapter of this book sets out to try to explain the phenomenon of the killer who mutilates by reference to two of the most noteworthy examples, Jack the Ripper of Victorian London, and Peter Kurten, the monster of Dusseldorf. It is highly unlikely that the identity of Jack the Ripper will ever be known. The confession of Peter Kurten does, however, throw much light on the psychology of a mass sadistic killer. It may be that Kurten can provide us with a number of clues to the personality and identity of the Yorkshire killer.

CHAPTER ONE

Murder, Horrible Murder

In 1887 Queen Victoria celebrated the Golden Jubilee of her long reign; a decade earlier she had been proclaimed Empress of India, the brightest jewel in the Imperial Crown. Britain maintained her industrial supremacy, confirmed as long before as the Great Exhibition of 1851, and the Port of London was the biggest and busiest in the whole world. The edifice of Victorian society looked as enduring, dependable and granite-faced as the Bank of England, and all the City monuments of Imperial industrial capitalism. Equally forbidding was the severe moral rectitude of Victorian society. Hypocrites they may have been, but their public face was as inflexible and stodgy as that of the monarch herself.

It was with considerable dismay, therefore, that the British public learnt news of a series of vicious and gruesome slayings which began on 31st August 1888. Not only did these serve as a source of ghoulish titillation and speculation, they brought to the public consciousness the horrifying barbarity of life within parts of the Imperial capital itself.

The Victorian system of public relief was so harsh that only *in extremis* would the poor enter the workhouse, there to suffer a regime of humiliation and degradation. For many, crime was an economic necessity.

One hundred years ago, in Westminster, Holborn and the East End there were said to be no less than 100,000 people living by crime. Thousands of women earned a living by prostitution. Such was the general promiscuity and lack of privacy that young children would simulate the sexual act openly in the street.

The East End of London gave an impression of constant movement. Pubs and clubs were open both early and late and drinking in the market areas would commence at 4 am when some of the pubs would be closing. Drunken sailors from Limehouse and the Port of London would penetrate as far as Whitechapel. The immigrant Jewish community was constantly threatened.

The explosive character of the East End had already been demonstrated in Jubilee year just before the Ripper murders when crowds of unemployed East Enders took to sleeping out in Trafalgar Square, finally to be evicted in November of that year by a large combined force of Grenadiers, Life Guards and Metropolitan Police.

The legendary crimes of Jack the Ripper reside in this historical background and are inseparable from it in the public imagination. So far as is known he was the perpetrator of a series of five ghastly crimes of murder and mutilation.

The following extract, which is quoted in Donald Rumbelow's book *The Complete Jack the Ripper*, is taken from a copy of notes originally written by Sir Melville Macnaughten several years after he joined Scotland Yard as Assistant Chief Constable in 1889.

Now the Whitechapel murderer had 5 victims – & 5 victims only – his murders were

(1) 31st August '88. Mary Ann Nichols – at Buck's Row – who was found with her throat cut – & with (slight) stomach mutilation.

(2) 8th Sept. '88. Annie Chapman – Hanbury St; – throat cut – badly – stomach and private parts mutilated & some of the entrails placed round the neck.

(3) 30th Sept. '88. Elizabeth Stride – Berner's Street, throat cut, but nothing in shape of mutilation attempted, & *on same date*

Catherine Eddowes – Mitre Square, throat cut & very bad mutilation, both of face & and stomach.

9th November. Mary Jane Kelly – Miller's Court, throat

cut, and the whole of the body mutilated in the most ghastly manner.

The last murder is the only one that took place in a *room*, and the murderer must have been at least 2 hours engaged. A photo was taken of the woman, as she was found lying on the bed, without seeing which it is impossible to imagine the awful mutilation.

With regard to the *double* murder which took place on 30th September, there is no doubt but that the man was disturbed by some Jews who drove up to a club (close to which the body of Elizabeth Stride was found) and that he then, '*mordum satiatus*', went in search of a further victim who he found at Mitre Square.

It will be noticed that the fury of the mutilations *increased* in each case, and, seemingly, the appetite only became sharpened by indulgence.

Sir Melville's theory is that

the murderer's brain gave way altogether after his awful glut in Miller's Court, and that he immediately committed suicide, or, as a possible alternative, was found to be so hopelessly mad by his relations, that he was confined by them in some asylum.

In every case the Ripper's victim was a prostitute. In addition there is strong evidence that drink was a common factor in all cases. Nichols, the first victim, had on the evening of her death staggered back from the Frying Pan public house in Brick Lane to her lodging house, but had been turned away because she lacked fourpence for a bed. Annie Chapman, part-time flower seller and prostitute, was well known as a frequent drunk. On the night of her murder she had set out to earn the price of a bed. Two weeks later, on the night of the horrifying double murder, Catherine Eddowes had been in police custody at a City police station. Some time after midnight she was let out of the station and with a : 'Night, Old Cock,' left to meet her destiny with Jack the Ripper. The other Ripper victim discovered that day, Elizabeth Stride, was also well known as a drunk. There is evidence too that Mary Kelly had been drinking on the night of her murder. Pregnant, she was desperate for money and was last seen at 2 am soliciting in the area of Thrawl Street.

There appeared no motive for these murders. In each case the victim was destitute. Even as prostitutes they possessed only the most limited physical attraction. The psychological motive would appear to be sheer sadism, an obsession with blood and dismemberment. A particularly macabre aspect of the Ripper case was a letter enclosing a small packet containing part of a human kidney which may throw some light on the corrupted mind of the murderer. The letter, which was addressed to Mr George Lusk, head of the Whitechapel Vigilance Committee, has been adjudged by an expert graphologist as likely to be authentic. The note was addressed 'From Hell' and read :

Mr Lusk
Sir I send you half the Kidne I took from one woman prasarved it for you tother piece I fried and ate it was very nise I may send you the bloody knif that took it out if you only wate a whil longer signed Catch me when you can Mishter Lusk

The kidney was examined by Dr Openshaw, the Pathological Curator of the London Hospital Museum and Mr Sutton, one of the senior surgeons of the London Hospital. Their findings seem to confirm in detail the assertion made in the grisly note. The kidney was 'ginny', of the kind to be found in an alcoholic, it belonged to a woman of about forty-five. It had been removed within the last three weeks and had been put in spirits. The kidney was in an advanced stage of Bright's disease and exactly matched the one remaining in Catherine Eddowes's body. As final proof of its authenticity it was discovered that a missing portion of the renal artery one inch in length remained attached to the kidney.

Ripper folklore spread quickly beyond the confines of the United Kingdom. It has in addition been constantly exploited by the live theatre and the film, radio and television media. It is always associated with a kind of nostalgia for a remote period of Dickensian poverty and characterisation, gas street lighting, coal fires and sulphurous fog. He is seen by some as a kind of social revolutionary, knife in hand, about to eviscerate the cancer of society.

In fact the social effects of the murderous year of Jack proved minimal. Social improvement came slowly. It was finally left to Herman Göring's Blitzkrieg to dispose of the Ripper's East End.*

It was the Germans who invented the word 'lustmord' which means murder for pleasure and enjoyment. The definition implies the enaction of extremes of perverted sexual fantasy where the victim is totally dominated and ravished.

Peter Kurten, German mass slayer and sadist, who was brought to trial in 1931, is certainly covered by this description, and it is possible to draw several lessons from his pattern of behaviour which may be helpful in an interpretation of the Yorkshire killer's psychology and motives.

Kurten had read accounts of Jack the Ripper several times. He also confessed to a love of movies depicting people falling from cliffs. When finally caught he was found guilty of murder in nine cases and attempted murder in seven. Less 'selective' than the Ripper, he killed or badly injured men, women, children, horses, sheep and even on one occasion when there was no other suitable victim to hand, a swan.

Kurten experienced a harsh and unhappy childhood. Among his youthful perversions were the torture of animals, particularly dogs. It is thought that at the age of nine he drowned two companions in the river. He began his criminal career of larceny mainly in inns or pubs where the landlord would be engaged downstairs in the bar and his Frau in the kitchen. He was in addition a pyromaniac specialising in the

*Incidentally the last attempted occupation of West London by East Enders took place in 1945 and was repulsed by the civil arm of the Attlee government.

burning of hayricks. He attempted on several occasions to set fire to the Dusseldorf Orphanage, but it failed to ignite.

After his arrest Kurten recalled his satisfaction with acts of arson :

When people dashed about screaming I enjoyed it immensely. The bright glow of the fire at night was exciting. During the firing itself the thought that human beings might be burned added to the sensations that I experienced. I always watched the fires, usually near at hand, so near in fact that I have been asked to give a helping hand. The shouting of the people and the glare of the fire pleased me. During big fires I always came to an ejaculation.

During his long terms of imprisonment for arson and larceny he frequently experienced spells of solitary confinement. It was then that Kurten sought to retreat into a world of morbid fantasy occupied by violent and perverted sexual imaginings. These imaginings were related to fire and blood. He recalled on one occasion how on his return to Dusseldorf the sky was blood red, which he took as a favourable omen.

Kurten's public *persona* was in no way indicative of his inner obsessions. He took great care of his personal appearance and applied both rouge and powder to his face which made him look younger than his years. So meticulous was he that exhaustive forensic investigation after his final arrest failed to turn up traces of blood except in pocket linings where he had carried weapons.

A photograph taken in 1930 reveals him as the epitome of lower middle class respectability. He was obviously acceptable as a husband, indeed when he told his wife the full catalogue of his crimes her immediate concern was that she would become an unsupported widow. With typical practicality Kurten responded by suggesting she should go to the police station and claim the reward money offered for his capture. Kurten undoubtedly had considerable charm for women and even those he had half throttled would on occasion agree to a further meeting with him.

Kurten clearly was a degenerate and sadistic psychopath though never insane to the point where he was no longer responsible for his actions or incapable of stopping them. Intercourse with his victims was only satisfactory for him when accompanied by the infliction of pain. Orgasm would frequently occur on the point of death of the victim or where slashing and mutilation occasioned an issue of blood.

Kurten's psychopathic character is shown clearly in his total lack of remorse for his crimes and his matter-of-fact description of them. After the murder of two girls he describes how :

On the following Sunday, the 25th of August, I went once more to Flehe to savour the effect of my crime. I listened to the various accounts given by the inhabitants, going from group to group of excited people, listening to them. It gave me pleasure that the lovely bright Sunday in Dusseldorf had been shattered as by a lightning stroke.

On another occasion he admitted :

I did have a constant desire – you will call it the urge to kill – and the more the better. Yes, if I had had the means I would have killed masses. I would have caused catastrophes. Every evening, when my wife was working late, I scoured the town for a victim. But it was not so easy to find one. The sexual urge was strongly developed in me, particularly in the last years, and it was stimulated even more by the crimes themselves. For that reason I was always driven to find a new victim. Sometimes even when I seized my victim's throat, I had an orgasm; sometimes not, but then the orgasm came as I stabbed the victim. It was not my intention to get satisfaction by normal sexual intercourse but by killing. When the victim struggled she merely stimulated my lust.

Kurten consistently demonstrated a total lack of feeling

or concern for the views of others. Towards the end of his final imprisonment, trial and investigation, Kurten displayed little sign of emotional human remorse and his thoughts led him to contemplate his execution by guillotine with equanimity and pleasure. His examining psychiatrist, Karl Berg, Professor of Forensic Medicine in Dusseldorf Medical Academy, recalled : 'Kurten asked me whether, his head chopped off, he would still hear the gushing of blood. That would be for him, he said, the pleasure of all pleasures.'

CHAPTER TWO

Chronicle of Death

Since mid-1975 the industrial towns of the West Riding of Yorkshire have experienced a series of terrifying and vicious murders on a scale Britain has not previously witnessed. So far there have been twelve murders in which horrifying mutilations of the victims have occurred. In almost all cases the murdered women have suffered severe head injuries and laceration of the trunk of the body. The victims have in the main been prostitutes, or, in the delicate phraseology of the West Yorkshire police, 'good time girls'. It is important to emphasise, however, that among his victims the Yorkshire Ripper has also claimed the lives of young and totally innocent girls.

Another distressing aspect of this case is the number of children who have lost their mothers. Admittedly some of them were already in local authority care, or with foster parents, but there were a number of others who were as well cared for by their mothers as circumstances would allow. Teachers and social workers will confirm that the children of prostitute women are frequently well cared for, at least from a material point of view. In all, no less than twenty-three children have been left motherless, and some have been orphaned completely.

From the start of their investigations into the epidemic of murder it was clear to the police that they were dealing with a ruthless psychopath. Detective Chief Superintendent Dennis Hoban (who died in March, 1978) stated at the inquest on Wilma McCann, the first victim : 'The pattern of stab wounds immediately brought to my mind the maniacal type of homicide that sometimes occurs.'

It has been the unenviable task of Mr George Oldfield (Assistant Chief Constable of the West Yorkshire Police) to head the inquiry, which to date has lasted more than four years. He has warned repeatedly that unless apprehended the murderer will kill again. 'He's crafty, he has given us the runaround for four years and he gets a kick out of it. He is brutal, calm and cunning, but he is driven by a terrible urge; when it overcomes him, he flips.'

Chapter One of this book attempted to illustrate by two historical examples the mind of a cruel psychopathic killer; it may be that as the grisly story of the Pennines murders unfolds the reader will be able to identify certain characteristics common to the cases already examined.

It should be pointed out that the narrative supplied herein is by no means exhaustive. For good practical reasons George Oldfield is unwilling to release precise details of the killings which might stimulate others to imitate the killer. There is, after all, more than one maniacal killer abroad in West Yorkshire and there were at one time thought to be as many as six. There are in addition always a number of 'loonies' willing to confess to a spectacular series of crimes; the greater their detailed knowledge the more likely they are to be able to interfere with police work. At least one case of a confession has already come to court where an alcoholic had sought to deflect attention from an act of arson by confessing to the Ripper murders!

Mr Oldfield stated in June, 1977: 'I believe I know the weapons that have been used, although I am not prepared to say what, other than that they include a blunt instrument.' We must therefore work on the assumption that the killer, like Peter Kurten, uses something like a hammer and a knife, but this does not exclude the possibility of an armoury of other weapons.

The inquiries are incomplete, no arrest has been made, there is no accused in the dock. Our investigations therefore must be inconclusive and speculative.

On the foggy evening of 29th October 1975, twenty-eight-year-old Mrs Wilma McCann put her four children to bed, changed into a pink blouse and cream skirt and left home for the last time. At 5 am, worried that she had not returned, her young family set out to look for her. Neighbours saw two of the children waiting at the bus stop hoping to see her step off the early morning bus. An hour later, milkman Alan Routledge on his morning round spotted what he at first took to be a bundle of rags on the bank surrounding the Prince Philip Playing Fields only a hundred yards from her home. It lay shrouded in mist. 'I thought nothing of it,' he recounted, 'and then my brother who was with me shouted, "It's a body!"' To their horror they discovered the grievously mutilated body of Wilma McCann. Her strawberry blonde hair was matted with blood, her head a mass of horrible lacerations and contusions, her breasts and stomach had been slashed open. The following day her children were taken into the care of Leeds County Council.

There then began an inquiry by the West Yorkshire police into what was to become the most gruesome and horrible series of murders Britain has ever known.

A petite woman in her twenties, separated from her husband, Wilma McCann was in the police description a 'good time girl'. She was trying, in straitened circumstances, to bring up a young family on her own in the seedy environment bordering on Chapeltown, Leeds. Little wonder, then, that she was attracted to the warmth and easy company of the boozy pubs and clubs of the city of Leeds. Before she left home on the fatal night she announced that she would be visiting The Scotsman, The Regent and The White Swan public houses, which are in the city centre. Closer to home Mrs McCann was well known at the Scott Hall Hotel, a 1930s Whitbread house where she is still remembered with affection. People there deny she was a prostitute, but admit that she had an unusually large number of boyfriends. Indeed, by mid-December the police announced that they had interviewed twenty-nine of her boyfriends, but that there were still many more that they wished to see.

Wilma McCann was seen late on the night of her murder carrying a plastic container of curry and chips which she had acquired at the Room at the Top night-club. At about 1 am Wilma was seen by a man in an MGB sports car. He told the police that she looked very drunk; in an effort to get a lift up to Scott Hall Road she had jumped into the path of this car and flagged him down. The driver was going in the wrong direction and continued his journey without her.

No further information about her movements was available to the police. The murderer had come and gone in the dark. All the West Yorkshire police knew was that he had used blunt and sharp instruments to perpetrate his crime.

Wilma McCann's early life was described by her mother, Mrs Betsy Newlands, who lives in Inverness. 'Wilma was a good girl. I brought up a family of eleven and they had a strict upbringing. Wilma had to be in by ten o'clock at night and when her father first discovered she was wearing make-up he took it from her and buried it in the garden.' At one time Wilma had worked at the Gleneagles Hotel, but when six of her brothers settled in the Leeds area she moved there and married an Irishman, Patrick McCann. Eventually they separated and Wilma looked after the children. Mrs Newlands, who rejects any notion that Wilma was a prostitute, also recalled the horror she had experienced since October, 1975. 'I can't get it out of my mind and with each new murder the whole past history is raked up again. Often I have Wilma's face looking at me from the TV screen . . . I shall not rest until the monster is caught and my daughter's name is cleared,' she declared.

Injured Women

It is now thought that the Ripper had begun his vicious attacks on women in July, 1975. His first two victims, Anna Rogulski of Keighley and Olive Smelt of Halifax, both survived, but their injuries were such that they were unable to give police any information which would lead to conviction.

Anna Rogulski, Irish born and thirty-six years old, had been left for dead in an alley in Keighley. So severe were her injuries that she received the last rites of the Roman Catholic church. Surgeons fought for twelve hours to save her. Her head was shaved for the operation, and when the hair grew again what had been auburn grew back grey. Anna Rogulski still fears that the Ripper may return to finish off the job.

The attack on Mrs Olive Smelt, housewife and mother of three, at Woodside Mount, Halifax, occurred a little over a month later. Mrs Smelt, who was walking home when the attack took place, recalled: 'As I walked down the street a man came up to me face to face and said, "The weather's letting us down, isn't it?"' She was then attacked from behind, which would seem to be the Ripper's usual technique. 'The next thing I remember,' said Mrs Smelt, 'is crawling along the pavement covered in blood and shouting for help. All I can think is that he didn't finish me off because a courting couple in a car happened to switch on their headlights.' Mrs Smelt believed her attacker had a Yorkshire accent. She took a long time to overcome her injuries. 'I was in hospital for weeks, and I'm still not right. I have blood pressure and I suffer from depression, and I have sudden strong feelings of antagonism towards men. For a long time I wouldn't sleep with the window open: I had this fear that he might come back.'

As both of his first victims survived, it is perhaps not unreasonable to assume that at this stage in his exploits the Ripper had not perfected his murderous technique.

So far as is known only two other women have survived the killer's attacks, Maureen Long in July 1977 and Marilyn Moore later the same year. Mrs Long has no real recollection of the attack upon her. She is able to recall a merry evening in the Bali Hai. The next thing she remembers: 'I woke up on a piece of waste ground in Birkshall Lane under a mattress.' Mrs Long, who was forty-two, sustained severe

31

head and abdominal injuries and was left for dead by her attacker. She had been at the Bali Hai disco at Tiffany's night club in Manningham, Bradford. As the police later reconstructed the attack, the Ripper had been sufficiently audacious to set upon her near a gipsy encampment. Before he had time to kill her he had been frightened off by the barking of the gipsies' dogs. However, because of the terrible injuries she sustained, Maureen Long was unable to give the police more than a sketchy idea of what had happened or a description of her attacker.

In 1979 Mrs Long decided to appeal against an offer she had received from the Criminal Injuries Compensation Board. She had been given £350 interim compensation, but described the complete offer of £1,500 as 'insulting'.

Marilyn Moore was attacked on 14th December of the same year. Marilyn, a mother of four, worked as a prostitute in the Chapeltown area of Leeds, and it is her recollection of the brutal assassin which forms the basis of the two Identikit pictures issued by police. Marilyn accepted a lift from a man who it is thought may well have been the ripper. 'He was good-looking and he knew it – he had a drooping moustache and come-to-bed eyes, but there was something hard, almost vicious-looking about 'im.'

The car stopped in Scott Hall Street, less than two hundred yards from where the mutilated body of Wilma McCann had been found. He walked round the car and struck her on the head with a heavy metal object, shouting 'dirty prostitute bitch.' Marilyn's head was fractured, and surgeons had to insert fifty-six stitches into her wounds.

In December, 1978, Marilyn Moore recalled the nightmare thirty minutes she had spent with the Ripper. She said, 'I can never forget that night. For the first few months all I could see when I closed my eyes was his face. Sometimes I wish he had killed me, it might almost have been better than the nightmares he has left me.'

In November 1975, a little less than a month after the murder of Mrs McCann, Mrs Joan Mary Harrison, a mother of two, was found dead, having been savagely attacked with blows about the head. She died some time between 10.25 pm on Thursday 20th November and 8 am on Sunday 23rd November when her body was discovered lying face down on the concrete floor of a garage in Berwick Road, Preston. The garage was at the back of a derelict house fronting on to Frenchwood Street. Her murder was not immediately related to that of Wilma McCann, but after discussion between the Lancashire and West Yorkshire police forces, both women were thought to have suffered at the hands of the same killer.

Mrs Harrison, a native of Chorley, was living apart from her husband and two daughters, one of whom was being cared for by her grandmother, while the other was in the care of Preston Social Services Department. Joan, who was unemployed and living on social security, was last seen alive leaving a house in the Avenham Street area to go to a night club. Police said that she was a regular visitor to town centre pubs, but a friend described her as a 'quiet' girl.

The body was discovered by Mrs Mildred Atkinson, who noticed a garage door flapping in the wind when she was on her way to get the Sunday papers at 8 am. 'The door was blowing open and I saw the body lying face down. There was a coat over her head and I saw blood on the ground beside her . . . I did not know it was a woman . . . I thought it may have been a drunk who had banged his head.'

The post-mortem was carried out at Preston Royal Infirmary by pathologist Dr John Benstead, who was unable to determine the exact cause of death or pinpoint the exact time.

Police issued a description of Mrs Harrison as she was last seen leaving home: 'She was wearing a light green three-quarter-length coat with an imitation fur collar, turquoise-blue jumper with a bright yellow tank-top over it, dark brown trousers, and brown suede calf-length boots.'

Mr David Keighley, a Preston landlord and Mrs Harrison's fiancé, confirmed that Joan had a somewhat Jekyll and Hyde existence. At home she was quiet and domestic – one of her last actions had been to trim the Christmas tree. However, Joan Harrison's nature seemed to change when she went out on the town at night and became a heavy drinking 'good time girl'. Mr Keighley told the *Lancashire Evening Post* that while he was trying to give the girl a stable home life Joan would sometimes go on the binge and associate with winos down in Preston's skid row. However, he stated: 'Joan never brought any boyfriends back here – she knew I wouldn't have it . . . we were very close, we were engaged to be married, and I bought her a ring. She had her problems but I was trying to show her the better side of life, like staying at home at night, sitting by the fire and watching television instead of fooling around the town.' Mr Keighley confirmed that the last time he had seen Joan she went out for a drink at 10.25 pm on the Thursday and by Saturday morning he had begun to get worried.

Eighty detectives from Preston County police headquarters at Hutton, the Task force and the Regional Crime Squad, became immediately involved in the inquiry. Detective Superintendent Wilf Brooks, second in command of Lancashire CID, said there was no obvious motive for the murder, but 'it appeared to have been a savage attack'. The contents of Mrs Harrison's handbag, including cigarette lighters, rings and some drugs for her asthma, failed to turn up despite extensive police inquiries, although the bag itself was found in a park some time later.

It would appear that Joan Harrison was a heavy drinker and not averse to drinking cider from a bottle in back-street derelict property. Police inquiries, it seems, were rather hampered by the 'blurred' memories of many of her friends and associates. Detective Superintendent Brooks said: 'Our inquiries have been made more protracted by the life-style of the woman's friends.'

The *Evening Post* reporter located some of these friends:

'Talking amid the stench of old meths, cider and sherry bottles, they did not want to speak ill of the dead. One of them, boasting a couple of black eyes, said: "Aye, we knew her all right. It was Wednesday when I last saw her . . . She used to come down here quite a bit for a drink and the rest." '

On the day she disappeared Mrs Harrison had been seen at the St Mary's Hostel for homeless men, where she had a voluntary job as a part-time cleaner. She used to help out washing up. On the Thursday she had left about lunchtime. The hostel's warden, Mr Ian Pinchen, said that Mrs Harrison had set off with some of the hostel's staff. 'They all went for a drink at the nearby St Mary's pub, and Mrs Harrison came back a little drunk . . . She had to lie down on one of the rest beds and I believe she left the hostel around 10 pm.'

Mr Pinchen recalled: 'Joan was a kind sort of girl, good-natured as a rule. She knew quite a lot of the residents. She had seen the rougher side of life. But Joan used to drink too much, that was the cause of many of her problems.' Poor Joan Harrison: an alcoholic, also hooked on morphine present in cough mixtures, which she consumed at the rate of eight bottles a day. Her health was deteriorating rapidly. She had made an appearance at Preston Magistrates Court in 1974 at which she pleaded guilty to stealing and to forging a drug prescription. She was described during the case as 'a complete wreck of a human being'.

Detective Superintendent Brooks later revealed that Joan Harrison had had sexual intercourse shortly before she died. As the inquiry proceeded the search for people who had seen her from the Thursday night onwards broadened. Thousands of people were interviewed, more than a thousand statements taken. Preston pubs and clubs were thoroughly investigated and the inquiry spread to long-distance lorry drivers who were thought to have passed through Preston on the relevant dates. Police even took four hundred saliva tests, given mainly by people in the Avenham area of town. Twelve ships were in Preston dock in the days prior to the discovery of Mrs Harrison's body. All sailors

35

were interviewed as the ships returned and foreign police forces contacted where necessary.

Mrs Harrison's funeral was held on 5th December at St Mary's Roman Catholic Church, Chorley, where mass was said by the Very Reverend Monsignor Charles Jackson. A detective representing the Lancashire Murder Squad attended the fifty-minute service. Among the wreaths and bouquets was a large cross of white chrysanthemums and red roses. The attached cards read 'With all our love and remembrances, Mum and Dad', and 'Good night and God bless, Mummy, Denise and Maxine'.

It might be as well at this point to place on record certain reservations which suggest that Mrs Harrison may not after all have been a Ripper victim. Obviously much has been made of the life-style of this woman, which in certain particulars bears a strong resemblance to that of a number of the other Ripper victims. The cause of death given on the death certificate is as follows:

a Haemorrhage and shock caused by
b Multiple injuries
Murder by Person or Persons Unknown.

This suggests injuries similar to those of the other Ripper victims for whom death certificates have not so far been issued (June 1979). From the start of their inquiry Leeds police have been anxious not to reveal specific details related to the murders, and Coroners' courts are unwilling to discuss the inquests or even to release information as to their outcome, which, it is believed, is covered by the formula 'unlawfully killed by some person or persons unknown'.

One puzzling feature of the Harrison murder is that the Ripper seems to have gone beyond his normal geographical range of activity. Also one forms the view that Preston is not so vice-ridden as the Ripper's more familiar haunts. Again there is the matter of the disappearance of Mrs Harrison's handbag: did she have it with her at the time of the murder? Was it taken by the Ripper? Could it have been taken after the murder and its contents stolen by someone else? It would appear from what we know of the Ripper's activities that there is no evidence of theft as a motivation for his crimes.

These reservations apart, the Lancashire police seem reasonably well persuaded that they are looking for the same killer as the West Yorkshire police. Detective Chief Superintendent Wilf Brooks returned from a Ripper conference in the summer of 1979 expressing cautious confidence that the different police forces were looking for the same killer. He stated his determination to keep up the pressure and to make maximum use of a tape-recording broadcast by West Yorkshire police in June 1979. He announced that prostitutes and winos were to be invited to Police Headquarters because the authorities believed they might not have heard the recording. 'We will be going into pubs and known hideouts to find them, particularly those active at the time of Mrs Harrison's killing,' said Mr Brooks.

Mrs Emily Jackson

On the morning of Wednesday 21st January 1976 the body of Emily Jackson was discovered in a cul-de-sac only a stone's throw from where Wilma McCann was last seen alive after a visit to the Room at the Top night-club, Leeds.

Mrs Emily Jackson, forty-two, married and mother of three children, was resident at Back Green, Cherwell, Morley. She occasionally helped her husband Sidney with his roofing business. In the evenings, however, she was wont to use his blue Commer van with a ladder on top for social purposes.

On the night of her murder Mrs Emily Jackson had been with her husband Sidney at the Gaiety public house in Roundhay Road, Leeds, but she had left him early to patrol the streets. Mrs Jackson did not return to the Gaiety car park and her husband left by taxi and went home about 10.30 pm. The Jacksons were a fun-loving couple. Mr Jackson attributes this to the loss of their son. 'We lost our fourteen-year-old son Derek – he died after he fell through a window at home about five years ago. When that happened we decided life was too short, we would live for today and not bother about the future. I don't think my wife ever really got over it. We believed in having fun while we could.'

Together the parents had set out to forget the tragedy by submerging themselves in the night life of Leeds. They were well-known in the pubs and clubs, and on the bingo circuit. It was also known that Mrs Jackson would frequently go out at nights on her own.

Emily Jackson's body was dumped, probably from her own van, on the outskirts of Leeds' city centre. It was thought that the killer then made his getaway in the same van. Superintendent Dennis Hoban said that she had the same kind of head wounds and other injuries as those sustained by Wilma McCann. There appeared to be no motive for the attack. 'We are looking for a very sadistic and possibly sexually perverted killer.' The police were determined to leave no stone unturned. Seventy task officers were set to work on the case and the Leeds public were deluged with appeals for help and information from the police at soccer and rugby matches, in cinemas and in bingo halls.

Mrs Irene Richardson

It was with the murder, a little over a year later, of twenty-eight-year-old Irene Richardson that the grisly pattern of murder finally became firmly established in the public consciousness. A Scotswoman from Glasgow, she was parted from her husband George and their two young children, who were with foster parents. She had been working as a chambermaid in hotels, and on the fatal Saturday in February 1977 she had booked a room in Cowper Street, Chapeltown, Leeds. She was last seen alive at 11.15 pm that evening when she said she was going dancing at Tiffany's night spot which is in the centre of the city. Her mutilated body was later discovered by an early morning jogger on playing fields near Roundhay Park, Leeds, with severe head wounds and lacerations of the throat and abdomen. Detective Chief Superintendent James Hobson, head of Leeds CID, said : 'It would seem that she had been taken in a vehicle either from the dance hall or from the area where she lived to Roundhay in the north of the city. I still have an open mind whether she was killed there or killed somewhere else and her body taken there.'

Her husband, George Richardson, denied that she was a prostitute : 'She was sick, she just could not settle down.' During the last two weeks of her life poor Irene Richardson seems to have been completely without resources and she had been living rough in a toilet block. George Richardson, a plasterer living in Liverpool, had last met his wife in London at Easter 1976. They had been trying to bring about a reconciliation, but one evening he returned home to find that she had left him.

Mrs Marcella Margaret Mary Walsh said she had lived opposite Mrs Richardson at the time when Mrs Richardson had been living with a chef in the merchant navy. The couple had apparently talked about getting married in January 1977 but soon after Mrs Richardson had left him.

Mrs Walsh said she last saw Mrs Richardson on Saturday 5th February when she had come to her room to pick up her belongings. She had told her she was going to Tiffany's that evening and had taken a key to let herself in later. This was the last time Mrs Walsh was to see her alive.

Patricia Tina Atkinson

On 24th April 1977 Patricia Tina Atkinson, also known as McGee, and a well-known prostitute, was found dead in her flat at 9, Oak Avenue, Manningham, Bradford. She was the mother of three children, all of whom had been taken into care. Patricia, a divorcee aged thirty-three, was five feet seven inches tall with dark brown shoulder-length hair. She was last seen alive wearing a short black leather jacket, blue jeans and a blue shirt, and was carrying a blue denim handbag.

Patricia Atkinson was the only victim of the Ripper to be found battered to death in her own bed. The body had been covered with blankets, the pillow was blood-soaked. She bore similar marks to the other three victims murdered in Leeds. Her death came barely two months after that of Irene Richardson.

Atkinson obviously had quite a reputation, and is remembered in the Manningham area as an attractive person whose clients came from many different walks of life. She is described as very friendly, with a beautiful soft open face in contrast to the rather hard look which characterises most prostitute women. A friend recalls her great generosity and the fact that she would level peg in a drinking session, buying her own rounds all evening. It may be that the *bonhomie* generated in the Carlisle pub led to her ensnarement by the Ripper. The landlord remembers that at about 10.15 pm she was somewhat the worse for drink and he was forced to refuse her any more. She was last seen outside the pub talking of going on to the International Club in Lumb Lane, also in the red light district of Bradford. When questioned no one could remember whether she went off with a man or not. The police recovered a diary with some fifty names, but none yielded a clue to her murderer's identity.

Detective Chief Inspector Domaille, Head of Bradford CID, took charge of the inquiry in which one hundred officers of the CID became involved. Bradford police made urgent appeals for information in three languages – English, Urdu and Punjabi.

CHAPTER THREE

Wall of Silence

It is something of a Yorkshire maxim that once you become involved with the police 'they are never off your doorstep'. One of the recurring themes of this investigation has been continued complaints by the police that the public has been unwilling to come forward with information. A persistent dilemma of police work is that the custodians of the law have to rely heavily on the advice and assistance of those sections of the community who are naturally antagonistic towards them. Nearly all the murders which are the subject of this inquiry occurred in the twilight areas of inner cities. Because of the low value of the deteriorating properties they house illegal drinking clubs, gambling haunts and a variety of criminal activities. Deprivation and vice go naturally hand in hand. In this case the police were additionally hampered by the character of the victims.

The difficulty of the police is illustrated by the statement made at the inquest into the fourth Leeds murder. Chief Superintendent Hobson, head of Leeds CID, told the inquest that in an effort to reduce prostitution in the Chapeltown area in the twelve months prior to September 1978, one hundred and fifty-two women had been arrested or re-arrested and reported for prostitution and a further sixty-eight had been cautioned. These women were obviously drawn from the very section of the community of the greatest potential value as witness to the murders.

It must be said of all five murdered women that their way of life exposed them to danger. It must be said also that their friends and acquaintances would be more than unusually reluctant to step forward to assist the police. The people of Manningham, Bradford and Chapeltown, Leeds, keep their eyes straight ahead and are not over inquisitive about the trade of prostitution carried out in their midst. It pays not to know. Prostitutes' clients make unwilling witnesses. Many of the prostitutes are transients, plying their trade in the towns of the West Riding and far beyond. As Mr Ronald Gregory, the Chief Constable of West Yorkshire put it, 'They work in a twilight area where no one wants to be known. Many prostitutes also lead a nomadic life. In Leeds one week, in Birmingham the next, then perhaps in Nottingham.'

Chief Superintendent Hobson pointed to another difficulty: 'Among the prostitute society some of them know of men who have been violent towards them. We are getting their co-operation and following up every instance of assault which is reported. One of the problems is that these girls regard being with men as part of their job and do not pay much attention to the identity of whoever they may be with. When they get in cars with men they will go to quiet places where nobody will see them and unwittingly create the perfect scene for murder.'

Ladies of easy virtue command little sympathy from the community no matter how gruesome their end may be. What public sympathy there was, was reserved mainly for the children of these lonely and unfortunate women. As Mrs Irene McDonald, mother of one of the later victims in this case, a completely innocent girl, declared, 'I feel if they had all been Sunday School teachers the public would have come forward with clues and the man would have been caught by now.'

In one of his many appeals to the public Mr George Oldfield asked, 'I would like to put these questions to the people who have not come forward: First, do they want us to catch the killer or not? Secondly, have they a wife, sister, daughter or girlfriend who could be the next victim? And thirdly, if something similar happened to someone near them what would they expect us to do about it?' On another occasion Mr Oldfield remarked bitterly, 'Life's becoming cheap. Fifteen or twenty years ago we'd have been holding the public back. So many would have been anxious to give us information. We'd have wrapped this one up by now. There are hundreds of potential witnesses, customers of the girls, who refuse to contact the police for fear of personal embarrassment, despite assurances of utter confidentiality. These men are stupid. It causes us enormous work, but when we eventually trace them we are having to call on them even if they are married.' These feelings about public indifference seem to be confirmed by the experience of local crime reporters who have found there is less public interest and concern for the crime of murder than in the past.*

In all there are estimated to be about two hundred prostitutes working in the Bradford, Huddersfield and Leeds red light areas. Some of them had by this stage been placed under a kind of unofficial curfew, and were not allowed on the streets after 7 pm. As one girl put it, 'I try not to think about the murders. I am terrified of what might happen, but I just keep going out. I have had difficult clients in the past and been in very nasty situations, but I try not to think about it.'

The fears of the girls patrolling the streets in the big north-western towns spanning the Pennines intensified. Robin Baxter of the West Yorkshire Metropolitan Police was quoted as saying : 'At least the murders have done away wtih the amateurs. The hard-core professionals see the danger as part of the job and just carry on.' One girl who knew two of the victims said, 'You've gotta earn a living, haven't you?' But, she admitted, she had bought a pickaxe to defend herself. 'I'm so jumpy these days, I'm beginning to think it isn't even worth a hundred quid a night.' Other girls armed themselves with knives, pins, pepper and other repellants.

*In fact the official statistics suggest that the murder rate itself has barely altered in twentieth-century Britain, remaining at about a level of 150 per annum. These Home Office statistics are open to a variety of interpretations.

CHAPTER FOUR

Triangle of Fear

The long arm of the Ripper has inflicted death, mutilation and terror in six towns in Northern England, from Preston in the West to Leeds, Bradford, Huddersfield and Halifax in the Yorkshire Pennines. The triangle is completed by Manchester in the South.

Most of the towns are or were textile towns specialising in cotton in the West, and in wool and worsted in the East. Now in common with many parts of Northern England they face industrial decline, rising unemployment, and many of the problems of urban decay associated with inner city areas.

Thumbing through the location notes which make up this chapter I am struck by the bitter criticism of so many of the towns involved. I would therefore like, in advance, to insert a corrective. My researches in West Yorkshire, Lancashire and Greater Manchester were, despite the morbid nature of the undertaking, a source of enjoyment. All the towns and cities visited have considerable architectural merit, and the whole region is distinguished by its friendliness and lack of vanity or affectation. All the towns involved reflect the peace, progress, purpose and permanence of a bygone era. They are well worth visiting. My bitterness is occasioned by the vandalism displayed by local politicians, inspired no doubt by the preposterous notions of planning officials, the arrogance of architects, the machinations of the road lobby and the pervasive greed in all these allied professions. Why should it be that property which has served five or six generations be replaced by slums less than ten years old and widely acknowledged to be unfit for habitation except by students and other 'sub-humans'?

It could be argued that the Ripper is one of the few beneficiaries of the planning process. Modern urban planning has brought the motorway into the centres of cities enabling the killer to surface in any of a dozen cities and disappear just as rapidly with little fear of being noticed or apprehended, and never being more than an hour or so's drive from home. The process of planning urban blight has of course helped to create the decaying areas where the Ripper reaps his terrible harvest.

The motorist enters the city of Leeds by a series of overpasses, underpasses, numerous roundabouts and finally, in the centre of town, a complex system of one-way streets. For the stranger it all comes as a rather nasty shock. Many of the fine, confident, massive Victorian public buildings still survive, but these are surrounded by acres of wasteland, one of the hallmarks of modern town planning. For a city untouched by aerial bombardment there does seem to be an enormous amount of more recent demolition. A large volume of traffic passes straight through the heart of the city which is as it were both bound and segmented by bands of concrete. It is difficult to avoid the impression that the Ripper has had a professional counterpart working in the municipal planning department. The feeling, unfortunately, is that the worst is by no means over yet. A mass of deep red brick factories and warehouses with shattered windows await demolition.

The four Leeds murders and one serious assault attributed to the Ripper have all occurred in the northern part of the city. The Scott Hall area where Wilma McCann lived is a late 1930s development of red brick terraced homes and well-tended gardens. The local, the Scott Hall Hotel, is a solid pub of the same vintage. Wilma McCann used it as her local, but, understandably perhaps, sought in addition greater variety and stimulus in Leeds' city centre.

Chapeltown by contrast is a much seedier nineteenth-century dark red brick terrace development. It bears the signs of successive waves of immigration from the days of the East European pogroms to the latest phase of West Indian immigration. As you walk up Chapeltown Road you can see the ethnic signposts of past eras. Here were the offices of the *Jewish Telegraph*, there stands the Ramgarhia Board, further up the Latvian Social Club and the Colony Club. The dominant social centre is the Hayfield pub which seems to typify life in Chapeltown. The saying is 'something 'appens in the 'Ayfield every bleeding night'.

On my visit my drink was upset by a rough-and-tumble between two young blacks. We then witnessed a powerful-looking Irishman put down on the floor three times by slaps on the head. A lady informed me knowledgeably that they were karate chops and shouted to the upright pugilist : 'Do me a favour, don't 'it that man any more.' She then settled down to discuss the Ripper. 'To my reckoning,' she maintained, with the obvious concurrence of a group of 'good time girls,' 'he is either a top policeman or a surgeon.' 'Of course it's all wrong,' she went on to say, 'God wants us all to die between clean sheets, not' – with a grimace – 'on the ground.'

As late as the 1950s J. B. Priestley observed that Chapeltown still retained 'traces of that restless glitter which is the gift of the Jew'. In today's Chapeltown this connection seems rather remote. Chapeltown is a part of the city which possesses very few open social facilities. Many of the clubs have closed down for one reason or another and such social activity as there is exists mainly in the streets or in pubs like the Hayfield. There are, of course, parties held in private homes. On the night of the murder of Jayne MacDonald, for instance, a party of forty people left the Strya Club in Chapeltown Road at 2 am to go on to a party in Sholebrooke Avenue.

It is small wonder that a large number of prostitutes or good time girls are attracted to this area.

There is no police station in Chapeltown, which you would think could do with one. The police have therefore had to rely rather heavily on the Panda car strategy. The concentration of the force into large Headquarters buildings has meant that beats have been extended and the public find the police inaccessible. Efforts have recently been made to get more men back on the beat who can make contact with the public and are more effective as a deterrent to crime and as information gatherers.

The Bradford police differ somewhat in their methods of operation. These differences are symbolised by the newly-built headquarters premises in each town. The Leeds Millgarth building exhibits a 'concrete fortress' style. Bradford, by contrast, has erected an enormous glass headquarters, Jacobs Wells, in the centre of the city. Whilst this suggests a more open approach to police work, community workers suggest that if anything it has produced confusion of roles and that less attention is paid to the professional police community officer than in Leeds. Bradford police are rather sensitive about their glass showpiece and people have been prevented from taking photographs of it. Some feel that there are certain positive aspects of the 'fortress' role Leeds police have assigned to themselves. Responsibilities have apparently been clearly defined, and careful attention is paid to the advice of their own community affairs officers.

An unfortunate case which has some bearing on the Ripper inquiry came up recently. Six months after George Lindo, a Bradford West Indian, was convicted for a betting shop robbery, Detective Constable Brearley, one of the officers investigating the case, was discovered to have forged statements from people he should have been interviewing in the Ripper case. In September 1978 Brearley resigned from the West Yorkshire police force. Lindo had maintained throughout that he had been forced to sign a confession, and had in addition a reliable alibi. On 7th June 1979, three judges sitting in the Appeal Court acquitted Lindo. The circumstances surrounding Lindo's arrest and conviction have done much to sour relations between the West Indian community and the Bradford police. The case also gives rise to concern about the effectiveness of police work, if forged statements of evidence have been manu-

47

factured for the Ripper inquiry.

In Bradford, research led me as usual to the seedier parts of town, centring on the run-down red light areas of the city, Manningham Lane and Lumb Lane. The pubs – the Barracks, the Perseverance and the Queen's – exude a warmth of hospitality. One of the locals of the Barracks, a male impersonator, recalls her professional career with Vesta Tilley, and also lays claim to a Lourdes miracle cure for blindness. Despite their friendliness, some of the local residents complained about the influx of immigrants and the general deterioration of the neighbourhood. Many of the mills and weaving sheds are vacant and derelict. Employment is hard to come by. Unemployment among immigrants is nineteen per cent and rising.

The big social centre is the Carlisle Hotel, run by a friendly and dynamic landlord who has on occasion given the police facilities to run a Ripper operations room at the rear of the premises. In the evening the pub is crowded and a number of very hardfaced prostitutes sit at the bar while shadowy ponces can be seen moving about like fish in water.

A curious feature of the policing arrangements was to be seen at the junction of Church Street and Bertram Street. Here on some railings outside a Pakistani shop lean three girls strung out like bait on a line. They certainly look very well protected by a ring of strategically-placed unidentified squad cars occupied by men and women police officers in plain clothes. One of the girls, Susan, described her job. She takes her clients behind the back of the shop for payment of £5, the client is allowed five minutes. Those with more expensive tastes are accommodated in a bedroom in nearby premises.

Apparently the girls are permitted on the streets at 7 pm and allowed to work until 11.30 pm. At one time Susan said that they used to carry knives, but the police have forbidden this. Susan, who started soliciting at the age of sixteen when she left the comprehensive school, is now an attractive eighteen-year-old. She spends most days with her mother and married sister, who gave up soliciting when she got married. She admits to being very scared of the Ripper, particularly because in one of the notes received by the police he is thought to have expressed the notion of returning again to the Manningham Street area where he has already killed and mutilated two prostitutes. So scared was she at one time that she took time off to go down to London to solicit in Bayswater.

In the special circumstances of this case there appears to be a co-operative relationship between certain prostitutes and the police. Shortly after the interview with Susan I was followed back to my hotel by Bradford CID officers. They informed me she had given them an account of the interview and that they had called to check my credentials. A number of journalists and television crews have come under police scrutiny, and have spent some time assisting them with their inquiries.

Manchester has a declining population of a little less than half a million. The Town Hall, a magnifiicent Gothic folly, stands in Albert Square. Facing it is a statue of John Bright in classical style, his figure representing the great Free Trade tradition of the city.

The Town Hall, whatever its grandeur, has ill-served the people of Hulme and Moss Side, a depressed area, a twilight zone of the inner city, which displays the disastrous failure of a social experiment. It was from Hulme that Vera Millward left to meet her death by the railings of the Royal Infirmary. It was from neighbouring Moss Side, contiguous with the vast Hulme Estate, that Jean Royle left her council flat; her mutilated remains being discovered some weeks later on an allotment not far away.

Paul Hannon of War On Want wrote in 1977, 'It is not necessary to go as far as South Africa to observe the reality of second-class citizenship. Deprived families, herded together, are to be seen in every major British inner city. Manchester's Hulme bears all the sociological characteristics of a Bantustan Reservation.'

If one walks into Hulme from the centre of town through subways under the motorways and the wasteland bordering them, one feels even on a sunny day a lowering of spirits. One also experiences a certain feeling of unease; after all, you will probably have been warned to stay away, or at least to exercise particular caution. The very inaccessibility of the area so near the city centre seems to produce a brooding atmosphere and an explosive potential for violence.

In October 1977 Councillor Allan Roberts, Manchester's Labour Chairman of Housing, stated in relation to the Hulme Estate that it was: 'An absolute tragedy, an unbelievable monstrous development – an unrelieved mass of concrete battleships jokingly called after famous architects. They are absolutely unbelievable, the environment is terrible and I cannot imagine how anybody could have possibly conceived them. Those people who did were designing housing accommodation for *other people* to live in and they did not take into account the social consequences of what they were doing.'

These sentiments were echoed in the same year by Councillor Tom Murphy, Manchester's Conservative Housing spokesman: 'There was no research into the social aspects of what they were doing when they built Hulme. The people there start drinking, some start taking tablets to settle their nerves and so it goes on. You cannot now find a member or ex-member of the City Council who will admit to having voted for the Hulme scheme to go ahead.'

Amazingly, when the scheme was first completed it won at least one architectural merit award. Like the Piggeries in Liverpool and some of the London 'slums in the sky', Hulme is among the worst examples of inner city deprivation and urban redevelopment. Nearly the whole community originated in slums elsewhere and there is very little social cohesion. Many of the dwellers who were transplanted *en masse* from Moss Side, Ardwick and Hulme itself carry with them a yearning and nostalgia for the old days. Hugh McCartney recalled for the *Manchester Evening News*:

The people of Hulme were a proud people, and, although poverty certainly existed, it was hidden in a stoic quality of independence and sincere neighbourliness that is today seldom seen.

The people of Hulme were a caring community and certainly nobody was ever lonely. There was always someone to pop in and have a chat, and if there was sickness, there would soon be a neighbour with a bowl of gruel or soup, or maybe a rabbit pie and other tasty offerings, given with goodness of heart.

The streets of Hulme were clean and tidy with rows of terraced houses standing proudly, their windows sparkling and decorated with lace curtains, and should any be frayed with constant washing, the edges would be tucked away hidden from sight.

The window sills and doors shone with their regular spring-cleaning and mirrored the character of their tenants, bravely ignoring the fact that there were no bathrooms, no hot water, no inside toilet and no electricity . . . '

In view of this it is little wonder that the new tenants of Hulme redevelopment plan originally welcomed their new circumstances, all modern amenities, up to 'Parker-Morris' standard. The astonishing fact is how quickly disillusionment set in. According to the Hulme People's Rights Centre report over sixty per cent of the population (in excess of 15,000) want desperately to move out of the area, yet Hulme has been completely rebuilt during the last decade.

Community leader Tom McClure confirmed for me the appalling conditions prevailing in Lindbeck Crescent. Only a few weeks before my visit a prostitute, June McDonald, had jumped to her death from the tenth floor of adjoining Medlock Court after a row with another prostitute. In the same block, in December of the previous year, a prostitute, Mary Jane O'Toole, was convicted of murdering, with forty-two stab wounds, a West Indian who allowed her to use his flat for immoral purposes. The man had a reputation for violence towards prostitutes, which may account for the relatively light sentence of five years imposed on Mary O'Toole.

Jean Royle, murdered by the Ripper, whose decaying body was found on Manchester allotments, lived at 204/18 Lindbeck with a man and her two children. She had taken up the tenancy in August 1977. A couple of months previously the then tenant, Amena Thorne, had already met her death in violent circumstances. A prostitute, she had apparently been picked up by an Austrian lorry driver who maintained that she had jumped from his moving vehicle. He was in the event found guilty of failing to stop and report an accident and of stealing Thorne's handbag which was left in the cab. The fine imposed – £140 (less than a week's wage for a continental lorry driver), was greeted with bitter resentment by Amena Thorne's relatives and friends. Her husband, who was in prison at the time, was allowed out under escort to attend the funeral.

In discussion with residents, it was put to them that these huge housing schemes, though obviously quite disastrous, were in fact well-intentioned mistakes. The tenants were unable to accept this. These entirely reasonable people attributed the scale of the architectural horror to 'money changing hands' and to malice on the part of the professional planners and architects involved. They regard the schemes as an attempt to isolate them from the rest of the community. The people feel trapped and marooned in what should be a prime area of the town adjacent to the city centre. When one looks at the tawdriness and squalor of the buildings and the way the estates have been sealed off by motorways, intentionally or otherwise, it is difficult to resist the conclusion the reesidents themselves have arrived at. One of the astonishing things is that Manchester is the only major city in Britain to have completed a slum clearance programme. As the Community Report put it, 'much of the damage that has been done is irreparable. Whole communities have been destroyed, and valium has replaced tea as a social habit.'

What of the local police? One would presumably expect

to see a healthy representation from the Greater Manchester Police force in an area where vandalism and crime are so rife. In the course of an admittedly brief, two-day visit to Hulme and Moss Side, I did not see a single policeman, but as I drove out of the city on the way south, I was to count dozens of uniformed men lining the route to the Manchester Show. What reasons other than 'cosmetic' they had to be present in such large numbers I am unable to suggest.

The following information is derived from a dossier entitled 'Inner City Crisis – Manchester's Hulme' produced by the Hulme People's Rights Centre. The people of Hulme:

> do not like this housing. There is no privacy; every little thing sounds through the paper-thin walls. The lifts are rarely working, and the rubbish chutes are invariably blocked. The cost of heating to counteract the damp and keep out the cold is astronomical. There is nowhere for the children to play in safety, nowhere for their mothers to go and make friends.

Mothers cannot let their children on to the landings. Some time ago a six-year-old fell five storeys to his death.

In short it is a disaster. A very expensive one, the cost of maintaining and repairing the properties being far, far greater than the original building cost ten years ago.

Hulme has acquired a reputation : its inhabitants are stigmatised. There is a high concentration of very poor people, the elderly and disabled, ex-homeless people with problems, a high incidence of alcoholism and drug dependence. Very many children leave school without any paper qualifications. Truancy and vandalism are rife. Hardly anyone wants to live in Hulme.

In the Crescents, perhaps the most notorious area, there are 916 dwellings (many of these are now un-occupied or taken up by short student lets). Of the remainder well over a third are occupied by single parent families and more than half by supplementary benefits claimants. In the deck access accommodation the effect of one anti-social family on their immediate neighbours is tenfold the effect of that on a traditional housing estate.

The incidence of vermin, vandalism and violent crime is far higher than in the pre-existing slum or any other comparable Manchester community. Certain statistics are thought to make Hulme almost unique in the United Kingdom. Taking the norm for Great Britain, you are, if you live in Hulme, seven times more likely to commit suicide, thirty-one times more likely to be the victim of crime, forty-one times more likely to be actually murdered.

In a discussion with Hulme residents I was told that conditions in Lindbeck Crescent, Moss Side district, an adjoining estate, were in fact worse. This was certainly confirmed by its external appearance. Inside, many of the dwellings are apparently crawling with black jacks (Northern word for cockroaches). Virtually all the garages are empty and vandalised, and the open car-parks are overgrown like Second World War airfields. There is a leisure centre at Moss Side, but locals say it is too expensive and is only used by outsiders.

To quote from the community report:

The relationship between the youth of Hulme and the 'Law' is nakedly hostile. No policemen live in Hulme. The police in Hulme are generally ineffective. Panda patrols are futile as three quarters of the crime is committed above ground level, only soliciting is exclusively at street level. When the police do appear in the 'streets in the sky', they arrive in threes and usually only to arrest someone.

At the access points, walkways, above ground stairways and subways

. . . no beat bobby is ever seen, yet every night, somewhere in Hulme, someone is mugged. An entire squad of fifty plainclothes men were drafted into Hulme with an anti-mugging brief, they remained six weeks and caught exactly one mugger. He confessed to seventy-two muggings, the majority of which had not even been reported.

At a recent committal for trial of a youth for the particularly brutal killing of an old woman, the Detective Superintendent who led the murder hunt publicly commented that it was the fault of the people of Hulme that it took four months to make the arrest. He went on to say, 'They just would not co-operate with us.'

Nor, on the other hand, it would seem, do the police place a high value on respect for the community in Hulme. One police sergeant is quoted as saying to workers at the People's Rights Centre: 'When you come to Hulme, you throw the book away.'

In a tape recording to be discussed later, the Ripper threatens to return to Manchester where he has already committed two murders. He claims to like Manchester because there are a lot of prostitutes about. One gets the feeling that this may be less true now than in the past. It is suggested that this is because of the strong moral posture of the Chief Constable, Mr James Anderton, a keen Methodist churchman. There is little doubt that the moral policy is effective from the sparse display on the newsagents' bookshelves. Large amounts of pornographic material have been sequestered by the police, whose indiscriminate enthusiasm has robbed the prurient reader of issues freely available in the rest of the country. The familiar 'executive' glossy magazines are difficult to obtain in Manchester. One bookshop has been raided thirteen times without a single prosecution being brought.

It is ironic that this moral drive does not seem to have followed through into concern for the safety of the individual citizen. Manchester's Judge Zigmond recently voiced criticism of the police after hearing of the amount of time nine city centre vice squad officers had spent observing a prostitute and her girl friend. He concluded that: 'With the crime rate we have today they [the officers] could be better employed patrolling the streets.'

Mr Anderton's moral enthusiasm may well have served to reduce the level of prostitution because a number of prostitutes, if sufficiently discouraged, can always be persuaded to move to another town. Nobody seems to know how many prostitutes there actually are in Manchester, though about four hundred is considered a reasonable estimate. Probably more than two hundred of these would represent an irreducible minimum prepared to risk arrest, court appearances and substantial fines – even imprisonment – to continue in their way of life. The *Daily Express* published an interview with one such, Jean, who reckoned to earn £70 per week to help her pay her way. 'We do no harm,' she said, 'some reckon we do good . . . You don't get many rapes in Hulme. They say it's because the fellows know where to go if they need something. They come to people like me.' She volunteered : 'Most of the kerbies have as much sex appeal as a tom cat. You never get Robert Redford pulling up on a wet night in the Princess Road, but at least it's the rent. Life must go on.'

The high-class tarts in Manchester's champagne bracket have more elevated aspirations than Jean or the Ripper's Manchester victims ever dreamt of. One girl told a journalist on the *Manchester Evening Review* that she makes sure to earn enough to send her daughter to a fee-paying school : 'I think education is so important, don't you ?'

Preston is an old town, currently celebrating its octocentenary. It is widely thought that Preston represents the Western limit of the Ripper's murderous forays.

Preston, in Lancashire, where Arkwright invented his famous loom, was once described by Daniel Defoe as being 'full of gentlemen, attorneys, proctors and notaries'. This impression no longer persists.

Approaching the town from the direction of Manchester one follows a road lined by a seemingly endless string of antique shops. It is as though the domestic heritage of Lancashire is being systematically crated up and shipped off to the Continent and to America. As Mr Jo Hoyles, well known local joke writer and sweet shop owner, puts it, 'Preston is more or less like a ghost town. Church Street used to be full of life, the centre of activity. Then they diverted the traffic. Now the shops must be struggling to make a living. There also seems to be a tendency to put up new buildings that you can't get into. It's like trying to worm your way into a tin of sardines.'

The scene of the Harrison murder, the Avenham Street area, consists of multi-storey and high rise flats (some as high as nineteen storeys) and fast-disappearing and very seedy Victorian red brick terrace property. The area lies to the back of Church Street, where Mrs Harrison used to drink in some of the pubs, and is closely adjacent to the town centre. Prostitutes still patrol in this area and in neighbouring roads such as Queen Street, London Road and Manchester Road.

It must be said that the police appear extremely vigilant, and shortly after commencing my inquiries I was to encounter CID officers Tingle and Darlington, with whom I had to establish my bona fides and explain the reasons for my researches. Returning to the Old Dog (no dogs allowed), Church Street, I was told that the pub had been cleaned up and all prostitutes evicted. It was said of this pub that Preston tarts would stand at the bar with price tags on the heel of their shoes. At the Wine Lodge up the street the landlord recalled having evicted Mrs Harrison, and claimed a considerable measure of success in having eliminated 'sin' altogether. There has obviously been something of a clean-up campaign.

Great Northern Street, in Huddersfield, scene of the Rytka murder, presents a picture of unrelieved gloom and dereliction which may be dispelled on market days, but which is certainly quite horrifying in the hours of darkness. Premises in Great Northern Street are mainly commercial or derelict, there is an empty Victorian school with broken windows at one end, and a public convenience at the other. The gents has long been known to the police as a favourite haunt of homosexuals. Opposite Garrards, the timber merchants where the murder took place, stands a large slaughter house. The pavement on either side of the road is horribly uneven and in the dark one is liable to step into pools of polluted water. The badly made-up street is broad and therefore well adapted to the 'car trade', enabling kerb crawlers to cruise slowly up and down.

Prostitutes, like newsvendors, have well-defined pitches where they can be identified by their customers. Helen Rytka is said to have had three such, outside Readymix Ltd in Leeds Road, the football ground in Leeds Road and Garrards Timber Merchants, Great Northern Street, where her fatal encounter with the Ripper took place.

There is now heavy police surveillance in the Great Northern Street area and prostitution is somewhat reduced. However, a number of girls still persist. A police constable recalled how even on the night of the horrifying discovery of Helen Rytka's body a young girl who knew full well of the tragedy took up her post in the pouring rain.

CHAPTER FIVE

'Sitting on a Fortune'

– Prostitutes' Saying

Most of the murder victims examined here were prostitutes though it is important to emphasise that this was not so in at least three cases. If it is true that the Ripper has a particular hatred for prostitutes, it may well be as well to examine the nature of prostitution and the lifestyle of its practitioners.

At the time of writing, prostitutes were being shot in Tehran by order of the Ayatollah Khomeini in an effort to cleanse and purify Iranian society. This illustrates the depth of feeling that prostitution can arouse in societies where it is regarded as a degrading indulgence. In our society prostitution is mercenary and despised, its practitioners are treated as a race apart. They are punished and blamed on the one hand, and paid generously on the other.

K. Davis, in his work on prostitution, asserts that the prostitute is indifferent not only to sexual pleasure but to her partner as well. This indifference reflects a pure commercialisation of sexual intimacy, and constitutes what Davis called the 'prostitutes' affront'.

According to Mary Riege Laner, the prostitute will frequently assume a pretence of intimacy; it is this, together with the sexual service, that the client seeks. In this sense prostitution is a crime without a victim, since the 'trick' is a party to the deception. He knows the prostitute is deceiving him, but he wants to believe in the deception and so participates in maintaining it.

Prostitution exists at all levels of society and the prostitutes themselves are drawn from all social groups.

Mary Riege Laner describes the life of prostitution as a 'vicious circle which spirals only downward. It is hazardous in terms of the law and of health. It is also psychologically hazardous since with increasing age and decreasing attractiveness always looming ahead, the prostitute is subject to an anxiety few other vocations produce.' The hazards of the profession often cause the prostitute to turn to alcohol and drugs for support. 'The combined effects of these supports, advancing age and unattractiveness or illness connected with the service the prostitute provides move even those who start at the upper levels progressively down the rungs of the occupational ladder into the lower strata of the profession. This means progressively less money and progressively more hardship.' Obviously in the slum areas of the northern cities one would expect to find a high proportion of prostitutes experiencing great hardship in the latter phases of their careers, which can in some cases go on into their sixties.

The basic function of prostitution is to provide a sexual service to people who fail to establish sexual relationships in a normal social context, or who find themselves more comfortable with casual relationships without any emotional commitment or dependence.

Mary Laner points out that prostitution also 'provides a service for businessmen in "entertaining" his customers, an adventure for the adolescent, an outlet for the single man (especially the physically unattractive one) and an outlet for the needs of the sexually abnormal. Since the transaction is essentially impersonal, prostitution can free the married man from emotional involvements and the public scandal that might result from adultery with non prostitutes. Prostitution to some extent protects ordinary women, particularly in places where large numbers of single men are concentrated. Prostitution may also function to sustain the sexual "conformity" of conventional women insofar as it reduces the pressure men might otherwise exert on them for nonconforming sexual behaviour.'

Most prostitutes are called upon in the course of their work to cater for a range of unusual requirements. To give two examples quoted by Wayland Young in his essay on prostitution:

A client used to come to me quite regularly. I had to undress and stand with my arms above my head. He took six kippers – he had them in pairs wrapped in cellophane, you know the things – and threw them at me one by one. If one of them missed he came trotting across the room and picked it up and tried again. Afterwards there was a pine-scented foam bath waiting for me. He went back to South Africa in the end. I was quite sorry. I used to get fourteen pounds a time.

And again:

A client took me back to his place, and as soon as I got in the door there was a dirty great coffin standing open. He put me in a white nightie with a rosary in one hand and a Bible in the other, and a wreath of roses on my head. Then I had to lie down in the coffin. I thought, 'Is this a gag to get my money?' But I had my bag in the coffin with me. Then he started nailing the lid down and all the time he was shouting out: 'You're dead now, God damn you to hell.' He'd told me his wife had died. He'd given me a big spanner to knock the lid up with, but I tell you I was wondering whether I'd ever get out again. I did, though, and when I looked round he'd gone.

Some 'kinkies' are very passive in their demands. For example, clients who just want the whore to dress up as a nurse and put them to bed with a bottle. Wayland Young points out that what most people would consider to be funny or disgusting stories are for the prostitute a matter of everyday existence.

What causes a girl to go on the game? A Leeds social

worker said that prostitutes originate in a certain type of caste or subculture in the city, girls from certain schools and certain definable home backgrounds, normally where there is an unstable parental relationship. The profession itself is quite mobile and it is observable in Leeds and Bradford, for example, that many of the women come from the North-East, Scotland and Ireland, as indeed did some of the victims concerned in the current investigation. Many of the girls originally left home to work in hotels or bars. Freed from family constraints and home support they begin to drift. A period of casual promiscuity may eventually encourage the girl to view herself as a commercial property.

A psychiatrist suggests: 'Past experiences may have tended to break down the prostitute's relationship to society or to make her feel that it had been broken down. In this way she is conditioned or made vulnerable to her environment . . . She may drift to a big city . . . She takes a job and finds herself in a stratum of society which encourages prostitution. She is caught in the hurly-burly of an indifferent city where the individual seems insignificant and she has little or no saving tie of affection with her family or anything in her past.'

Most delinquent girls give money as the main reason for going on the game. For example, Jean, a Chapeltown prostitute, stated: 'My reason is because I need the money I am working for on the streets. I mean, I only get a few pounds off the Social Security, not very much. After I've paid my rent, and bought some food I haven't got no money to buy clothes for me or my daughter, and my daughter's growing all the time, and she needs new clothes, you know.'

Susan in Bradford also gave money as her main reason, in addition to 'meeting interesting people'. One gains the impression that whilst the economic incentive is obviously very compelling, the girls may emphasise the importance of money for other reasons. High earnings reflect a girl's attractiveness, and no doubt boost her esteem in prostitute circles. This may in some measure compensate for the low self-valuation girls put on themselves. Also money offers a compelling reason which does not demonstrate a girl's personal inadequacy and perhaps her inability to work with others or to form satisfactory personal relationships.

Prostitutes often seem self-deluded, and many of them are heavy drinkers. As purveyors of illusion they themselves become deluded. Most prostitutes take a keen interest in the pageant of life rather than in notions of purpose, creativity or fulfilment.

Many girls are introduced into prostitution by friends, sisters or older women. The notion of the ponce as a professional corrupter appears ill-founded. Christine, a Chapeltown prostitute, said on London Weekend Television: 'I started going around with a friend who was already hustling, and she used to come up and use my place, and one night she brought up a client who wanted two girls and she asked me if I wanted to join in and I said no at first. And he said that he'd give me eight pounds just to sit there. So I sat there and he gave me eight pounds and it was a lot to me then. It just all started – I started walking around with her then and going and picking up clients.' Christine also referred to the migratory nature of her work: 'We travel from town to town, like when Leeds gets hot and the police, or there's nothing doing round here, you just take off to another town. You work in another town, stay in an hotel. If it gets hot there, you're off back to Leeds, stay in Leeds a week, move back, you know. Wherever you're going. It's just a lot of the girls tell you, if they've been out of town or it's been a good week then it gets around all the girls start going. It'll probably get hot down there 'cause there's too many girls going, you just move about again.'

In the Bradford, Huddersfield and Leeds red light districts there are estimated to be about two hundred women engaged in prostitution. For these women the Ripper, or 'Jackie' as they call him, poses an additional threat to their already hazardous lives. Many of them boast wounds inflicted by clients, they are all afraid of disease and like all social outlaws they seek to avoid contact with the police and are embarrassed by inquisitive questioning. One girl said, 'I'm terrified of what might happen, but I just keep going out.' Another said, 'When the Ripper's struck it makes you more aware of what you're doing, you'll probably work with another girl for two or three weeks and then when things cool off you'll start working on your own and forget all about it again.'

In Manchester, where the Ripper promised to strike next on the chilling tape released in June 1979, there are about four hundred prostitutes operating; about eighty of them patrol the Hulme Bullring area. Manchester police held meetings warning the girls of the Ripper danger, but many did not attend. As one girl put it, 'A policeman can't hold my hand in my kind of job, but I'll be looking out for myself. I'd be a fool if I said I wasn't a bit frightened.'

Most of the girls encountered in this survey did not appear to have a ponce or protector. In most cases the pros seemed to favour private enterprise. Ponces do however undoubtedly exist. In fact, certain women feel the need for a ponce in order to advance their self-esteem. The ponce can give some kind of structure to their lives, and if the prostitute is able to keep him affluent and well-dressed her credit goes up in the eyes of her colleagues.

CHAPTER SIX

Dossier of Murder

Jayne MacDonald

It was with the sixth killing that the public mood changed. On the weekend of 26th–27th June 1977 an innocent sixteen-year-old girl was battered to death. On the Sunday the body of Jayne MacDonald, a Leeds shopgirl, was found at 8 am by children playing in an adventure playground a quarter of a mile from her home. A boy of five recalled in a statement to the police: 'I saw a body on the ground so I told the others. There was a brown bag about four strides away and I did not touch her. I told a man in Reginald Street about the lady. I told him the lady was dead. We went up to the shop and told a man there what we had seen.'

The previous evening Jayne had set out for a disco in Leeds' city centre with her boyfriend. They went to the Hofbrau Haus, a disco pub, and Jayne saw him home. The boyfriend, Mark James, told the Leeds inquest that they had left the pub at closing time and had walked to his home to see if his sister's car was there, so he could drive Jayne home. As there was no car they went and lay in a field for three-quarters of an hour and then walked to Becket Street where they parted. It was then, presumably, that Jayne made the fatal decision to take a short-cut home through the vice area of Chapeltown near the Hayfield pub. Jayne lived only seven doors away from the killer's first victim, Wilma McCann.

In the words of Jayne's mother, Mrs MacDonald, 'Jayne was a very bonnie girl and drew boys. She had a trim figure and had lots of boyfriends, but she was innocent.' It was, quite naturally, her very youth and innocence which added so much to the sense of public outrage which greeted news of the crime. Gallows were painted on walls demanding, 'Hang the Ripper,' and petitions were got up for restoring capital punishment.

This was the first time that George Oldfield took charge personally of the Ripper investigation. Jayne's body had been found in the adventure playground off Reginald Street. From marks on the grass it was deduced that she had been dragged to the spot after being murdered in the street. A neighbour said she had heard banging, scuffling and a man with a Scottish accent shouting obscenities at the time of her death. Mr Oldfield threw every available man into the inquiry. From his knowledge of Chapeltown he knew that Reginald Street was a busy thoroughfare all night. George Oldfield's men found three hundred and eighty people who had been in Reginald Street that night. Only twenty people who had been seen by witnesses were never traced. The police assumed that most of these were either punters or prostitutes, but unfortunately they must have included the killer. Of the twenty, only one had been seen standing near the adventure playground at the time Jayne died. By description he was a strongly built white man. Exhaustive inquiries unfortunately failed to yield any more detailed description of the killer. Within weeks the killer had struck again, this time in Bradford, in a vicious attack on Maureen Long, which did not prove fatal, but in which she sustained serious head injuries.

Jean Royle

In October 1977 a young twenty-one-year-old woman, Jean Royle, also known as Jean Jordan, was killed in Manchester. The body was found about a mile from the M63 which links with the M62 trans-Pennine route and the Leeds and Bradford areas. Police encountered the now familiar difficulty in tracing the victim's movements during her last hours of life. Jean Royle had walked out of her council flat at Linbeck

Crescent, Hulme, Manchester, at 9 pm on Saturday, 1st October. It was not until noon on 10th October that her naked and mutilated body was found on a Manchester allotment next to Southern Cemetery at Chorlton-cum-Hardy. This is a place popular with courting couples, and where prostitutes took their clients. At the inquest in May 1978 Dr Reuben Woodcock revealed that the victim's head was blackened and she had been smashed eleven times by a heavy weapon with a rounded edge. She had knife wounds from the left shoulder to the right knee. There were eighteen wounds on her stomach and chest and another six on her right side. Some of the wounds were eight inches deep. There were no signs of sexual assault. At the inquest the Coroner, Mr Roderick Davies, said, 'We can assume she was knocked unconscious and whoever committed the crime ripped her up. It was a revolting case in which the belly was ripped open.'

Detective Chief Superintendent Jack Ridgeway, Head of Manchester CID, called in Vice Squad officers to contact all known prostitutes. 'The prostitutes who use that patch could tell me a lot,' said Mr Ridgeway. Cooperation, however, proved difficult to obtain. In Ridgeway's words, 'We have got her leaving home at 9 pm on 1st October. After that there is a brick wall. Nobody seems to have seen her from that moment until the body was found. There is a complete vacuum – there is no way that the body could have been in the position where it was found for nine days. It would have been seen.'

As Mr Ridgeway's words to reporters began to sink in they began to appreciate the macabre implications of his statement. Forensic evidence confirmed that Jean Royle died on 1st October. It also revealed that the murderer had returned to the corpse eight days after the killing, conducted further mutilations on the body, and dragged it from its place of concealment to a position more open to public view.

The murder of Jean Royle at Chorlton, Manchester, brought yet another police authority into the inquiry and illustrated one of the difficulties confronting the West York-shire police. At the Manchester inquest the Coroner allowed the Press to make public detailed evidence given by Dr Reuben Woodcock, Home Office pathologist, the nature of which West Yorkshire police had been most anxious not to disclose. In an effort to 'rectify' the situation a West York-shire police spokesman issued the following statement: 'It is the Greater Manchester police's investigation, not ours. We have cooperated, but it is still not our responsibility. All that has been given out are the details of one woman's injuries. It would be wrong to assume that other killings have happened in the same way.'

The murder scene yielded one clue which at the time seemed to offer great promise. A £5 note was discovered in Jean Royle's handbag, which it was thought she might have received as payment from her murderer. The note, number A.W. 51121565, was one of a batch of sixty-nine con-secutive numbers. The police launched a massive appeal to workers in Bradford, Shipley and Bingley to check their wage packets for £5 notes with a particular serial number. They even appealed to wives to examine their husbands' wage packets, despite the fact that such probing would be likely to be unpopular.

Chief Superintendent Ridgeway said in his appeal, 'I think it is extremely unlikely that the note could have crossed the Pennines in the normal course of business in just a couple of days. With Christmas approaching I am banking on the thrifty Yorkshire folk who have been putting money away. I would like them to look in their purses and wallets, and wives to look in their husbands' wallets and see if they can find any of the notes from the same bundle ... we will then know which firm the money was issued to.'

Jean, five foot six inches tall, and slim, weighing only seven-and-a-half stone, had dark auburn shoulder-length hair. She had come from Motherwell in Scotland and had met up with Alan Royle at Victoria Station, after she had run away from home. He recalled, 'I didn't even know she was a prostitute.' On arrival in Manchester some years later with her two young children Jean contacted the Homeless Family Unit. One helper who met her at this time remembers her as a quiet person (a description applied to more than one of the Ripper's victims). She dressed modestly and not in the brassy style favoured by some prostitutes. She was found accommodation at 204/18 on the notorious Linbeck Cresent, where she lived with an unemployed bingo worker, and a baby-sitter. She is remembered by a neighbour, Mrs Patricia MacFarlane, who confirmed that she was a quiet person and who told a *Manchester Evening News* reporter, 'She was definitely not the sort to talk to strangers in the street.'

At the Royle inquest the Coroner's Court was told that Jean had planned to give up her life of vice. Coroner Mr Roderick Davies read out a statement from a 'vice girl' called Anna Holt in which she said that she had 'worked the same patch' as a girl she knew as Scotch Jean, and had taken clients to the same flat. The statement added, 'she was trying to settle down to a normal life.'

On the night she met her death Jean Royle announced that she was going out 'to get a breath of air'. It is thought that she may have intended a visit to the Nile Club or the Reno Club or the Big Ally (Queen Alexandra public house). These premises have a poor reputation with the police and have in the past been known as haunts for prostitutes and drug traffickers. The streets immediately adjacent, like Broadfield Road, Raby Street and Westwood Street, are well-known to be frequented by prostitutes even in the daylight hours. It is thought that in any one of these Royle could have met the Ripper. The area contains a park, derelict property, back alleyways and vacant industrial premises, all calculated to offer maximum opportunity for the Ripper to carry out his murderous perversions.

As late as June 1978 Greater Manchester police had seventy detectives working on the case, and no less than nine thousand people had been interviewed. 'The morale of our officers is high and confident,' proclaimed Detective Superintendent Catlow, adding, 'I personally don't believe that we have yet met the killer in our multitude of interviews. When we do I'm positive we will realise and nail him.'

Helen Rytka

In 1975 the *Yorkshire Post* published a sad and emotional poem which turned out to be woefully prophetic in content:

Loneliness is to live in a world
Where people do not care.
Loneliness is to go outside,
To find no one is there, and
You fall down in despair,
Falling on your knees in prayer.
Asking God to rescue you,
From this cruel snare,
But no one comes
No voice is heard.
No one cares if I was lured.
Lured into the deepest hole,
Cast aside by those so cruel,
And treated like a mule.
Yes!
Loneliness is to live this way.
Day after day.
Yet I would pray
So that some day,
Love may find an open way,
Unloved is to miss the love
That all parents should give.
Yet they cast you aside
Put you out of their minds.
They put you in care.
There is no love there.
Yet the staff really care
Or they wouldn't be there.
Yet I know I shall die,

As my years drag by,
Oh, Why was it me, Lord?
Why?

The poem had been written by twin sisters of mixed blood early in the career of the murderous Ripper. In February 1978 the killer was to claim one of the sisters, Helen Rytka, as his eighth victim. By now Helen Rytka had become an eighteen-year-old prostitute, whose passion and strong ambition was to become a singer of soul music. She had apparently turned to prostitution to earn enough money to break into the pop world. She lived with her sister in a tiny bedsit high up above the Ring Road near a Sikh temple.

The sisters, who had spent most of their lives in care, had a very close relationship, so Helen did not die as lonely nor as friendless as many of the victims the Ripper had extinguished. Her sister Rita appealed for information on Yorkshire television : 'I could have lost nothing dearer than Helen,' she said. 'Nothing closer to my life could have gone than Helen. For his own sake and the public's sake, he [the murderer] should hand himself over. I knew the Ripper was in West Yorkshire, but you don't expect it to happen to you. It just happened to Helen.' Rita said she and her sister had been really close. 'We had a psyche [sic] between our minds. If she had a problem I knew I could feel it.' She also talked of how she was going to get over Helen's death : 'I am still young. I have my whole life ahead of me. I have to survive.'

Mr George Oldfield, Head of West Yorkshire CID, again appealed for witnesses, in particular the two men who had earlier picked up the Rytka sisters. Both men were later eliminated from the inquiry when it was learned that Helen had returned to Great Northern Street to resume her beat. Mr Oldfield appealed for more information.

In the meantime the Chief Constable of West Yorkshire stated on Independent Television that the Ripper had no hope of stopping prostitution if that was what he was attempting. By now even the most hardened of West Yorkshire prostitutes had become seriously alarmed. One was quoted as saying, 'If I carry on with the game I won't be working by myself. I'll stick with a friend.' In fact this had been the practice of the Rytka sisters, but it had not, unhappily, afforded Helen any protection.

A television programme on the Yorkshire Ripper produced by London Weekend's 'Weekend World' team offered a fascinating reconstruction of events on the night of the Rytka murder. It was screened on 8th October 1978 and had been produced in close cooperation with the West Yorkshire police. The following extract is derived from the television investigation:

Reporter Hugh Pile –
Helen and Rita were working in parallel, monitoring each other's movements. They'd each accept clients at the same time. They'd each give them a precise twenty minutes. And afterwards they'd each attempt to rendezvous at the same moment at the same place – a block of public lavatories. On the night that the murdered girl had died, the plan had worked well for the first half of the evening. At ten minutes past nine the sisters had set out simultaneously with their clients. But then the plan had begun to go badly wrong. When Rita had returned to the lavatories on time at nine-thirty her sister was nowhere to be seen. And as a prostitute Rita was sufficiently scared of the police not to report her sister's disappearance until three days later. George Oldfield was presented with the problem of having to reconstruct the murdered girl's movements after she had left Rita at 9.10. He succeeded in finding the client she had taken at that time, and his recollection of what had happened showed why the girls' safety plan had failed.

The murdered girl had been early at the rendezvous. With the client she had returned to the lavatories at 9.25, five minutes before her sister. But after the client had dropped her she had walked away. He'd never seen her again, and he'd certainly not seen her killer. But George Oldfield still saw a glimmer of hope: because the murdered girl had disappeared relatively early in the evening there were still plenty of people about, both on foot and in cars. He hoped some of them had seen the killer. His men traced and interviewed more than a hundred of them. And they accounted for all the cars in the street except three. George Oldfield's men never succeeded in tracing these cars. They concluded that they may have been driven by homosexuals who also often used the lavatories for a rendezvous. Because they, just like the prostitutes, would have been frightened of the police, they'd probably decided not to talk to them. That left just one other line for George Oldfield to follow. One person who'd been passing in a car told police he'd glimpsed a man lurking near the lavatories. The man had a stocky figure and light-coloured hair, but George Oldfield's men never succeeded in tracing him, so they never found out whether the man was another possible witness or the killer himself. He'd vanished into the dark.

At the Rytka inquest of 2nd February 1979 Mr Peter Gill, the Kirklees Coroner, said, 'If only the full details could be revealed they would shock even our modern society.' What is known of the Rytka murder is horrible enough. On a visit to the scene of the crime I was shown the rear wall of a hut where Helen was murdered. The foreman of Garrard's timber yard, Mr Melvin Clelland, told me about the day the body was discovered. 'One of the young drivers who was here on the Thursday found a pair of women's blood-stained knickers in the yard but we thought nothing about it: it's the area for prostitutes and many of the girls take men through the yard . . . I remember sitting here the following morning and remarking on the noise the birds were making. I said spring must be coming early this year.' Sadly the birds were not harbingers of spring, but heralds of death. 'The first thing we knew,' continued Mr Clelland, 'was at 3 pm when the police rang up and asked for permission to search the yard . . . two men arrived, one released his dog which went straight to the body, the policeman took one look and said, "This is it — stay away!" '

The body was found concealed in a gap between a disused garage and a high stack of timber. Police arrived in droves and began their search on hands and knees in the pouring rain. In January darkness came quickly and police, working late into the night, removed the body some time after midnight.

I have had described to me the way the murder is thought to have taken place. It has not, however, been possible to obtain official confirmation at this stage of the theory or its implications. Helen Rytka is known to have been murdered by the rear wall of the foreman's shed. This was spattered with blood, which is entirely consistent with severe skull injury. At some stage the body was stripped and removed a few yards from the actual point of murder to its place of concealment behind a high stack of wood planks. The suggestion made to me is that forensic examination revealed a considerable impregnation of the ground with blood, and that this could only have occurred if the body had been left lying at the point at which death happened. The provisional conclusion which has gained some acceptance is that the Ripper left the corpse lying where it fell and returned some hours later whereupon he conducted further mutilations. Helen's clothing was dispersed over a fairly wide area, and her shoes, it was discovered, had been thrown some seventy or more feet up a railway embankment at the rear of the timber yard. In order to conceal the body in the place it was found, it would have had to be lifted over a large stack of timber, which would indicate very considerable strength on the part of the killer.

If the theory as outlined is correct, what does it reveal of the nature of the killer? In the first place it does suggest a high degree of nerve. If the killer was disturbed, he did not panic to the extent of being unwilling to return to the scene of the crime. Helen Rytka's sister has told that she knew Helen to be missing within minutes of her disappearance; it is quite possible that at any time thereafter her disappearance could have been reported to the police, and that the Ripper could have been apprehended on his return to complete his evil deeds. The killer most probably did not know this, but he must have been aware of the appalling risk of capture he was taking. Almost certainly blood-spattered, probably carrying a weapon, he would have had to return to his car in a lit street, then either drive around, wait in a secluded spot, or drive home, before returning to the scene of the crime.

Should the above interpretation of the murder scene be correct it would suggest that the killer's main instinct is sadistic. Whatever impulse precipitates his attacks on women, the motive which impels his return to the scene of the crime appears to be pure necro-sadism.

At the inquest the coroner warned once more that the killer could strike again. Unfortunately the bitter trail of blood and savagery had not yet reached its end.

Helen Rytka's funeral was held at St Anthony's Roman Catholic Church, Bradford. On one wreath there was a tribute which read

To My Dearest Daughter Elena
With Everlasting Memories
from
Mother and Family

Perhaps it was the sheer accumulation of horror and the shock of the awful death of Helen Rytka that made the West Yorkshire Police Authority decide to offer a cash reward for information leading to the conviction of the killer. The Home Office had been approached previously on the matter but in its wisdom chose not to respond to the request from the police authority. The Ministry view is not an unreasonable one : rewards offer a strong temptation to form vigilante groups. In the past promise of reward led to the formation of blood money conspiracies and the framing of innocent men. In 1772 this resulted in the execution and imprisonment of several innocent people; the last blood money trial was held in 1816. In any event a £10,000 reward was offered in February 1978. This figure was doubled in the same year. The *Yorkshire Evening Post* and the *Yorkshire Post* have offered a further £5,000. In fact, enthusiasm for even high rewards was demonstrated by a 'Catch the Ripper' fund distribution of 200 collection boxes to pubs and clubs, organised by the Reverend R. Simpson, Vicar of St Marks, Woodhouse, Leeds. In a statement to publicise the official reward fund, Councillor Kenneth Davison, Chairman of the West Yorkshire Police Authority, has said, 'I would prefer him alive, but if I could not get him alive, I would want him dead.'

Yvonne Pearson

The next victim was discovered near notorious Lumb Lane in the red light district of Bradford. Yvonne Pearson was in fact probably killed before Helen Rytka, but her body was not discovered until after the Rytka killing. In March 1978 a man walking across a patch of waste land behind Lindfield Auto (Bradford) Ltd saw an arm stretching out from beneath an upturned settee. Superintendent Lapish was reported as saying that it was a possibility that the killer could have come back some time after the incident to move the settee to expose the body. The corpse, half naked and badly decomposed, bore all the marks of a Ripper killing. The victim, Yvonne Pearson, had disappeared on 21st January after leaving her two young children, Colette and Lorraine, with a babysitter. She was due to appear at Bradford Magistrates' Court on 26th January on charges of soliciting.

According to a neighbour and personal friend of Yvonne, she was afraid, as she put it, of being the next one to go. 'It would be just my luck to get knocked on the head,' she said. She was by all accounts a good friend and neighbour and she is said to have had the best-dressed kids in the whole street. She was apparently badly in debt at the time she was murdered.

The police made their now familiar appeal for information. A police spokesman admitted, however: 'Perhaps it is because the murders are so common, I think the general public may be getting a bit shell-shocked. The people who knew her were either in the same business or were clients and it makes them reluctant to come forward.'

Pearson had an address book which led police to believe that she travelled a nationwide network of prostitution. To avoid personal embarrassment the police gave those listed in the book thirty-six hours to come forward voluntarily with information, but most did not. Apparently Yvonne had clients with special tastes. There was one who wanted to be burned with a cigarette end. Again, in this case, the killer had attacked a lonely prostitute in an area well known to be frequented by 'punters' and good time girls. There is also the suggestion that, as in the case of the Royle killing, the murderer returned to the scene of the crime possibly to expose the body. This would suggest that the killer may crave publicity for his actions and would lend support to the theory that his aim is to conduct a well-publicised moral crusade against prostitution.

Mrs Vera Millward

This theory is reinforced by the circumstances surrounding the murder of Vera Millward, forty years old, mother of seven children and common law wife of a Mr Cy Burkett. She left home about 10 pm and was found the following morning stabbed in the stomach and clubbed viciously to death. Her body was found propped up against a fence behind the Manchester Royal Infirmary. One of a group of workmen who discovered her said, 'At first I thought it was a doll, then I realised it was a body. It was a terrible shock!'

By now the total killings had doubled the fearful toll of the macabre series of deaths inflicted by the original Jack the Ripper in the streets of London in the 1880s.

The pattern of the killing reproduced that of many of the earlier murders. Again the victim was a prostitute. She had in fact been waiting for a regular client at a pre-determined venue. He had failed to keep his appointment. The injuries bore all the marks of a Ripper killing. Chief Superintendent Jack Ridgeway, Head of Greater Manchester Central Crime area, held a joint Press Conference with Detective Chief Superintendent John Domaille, then in charge of a newly-formed police Ripper team in West Yorkshire. Ridgeway stated: 'She was killed by blows to the head with a blunt instrument, and she had abdominal injuries which were done with a sharp instrument, different from that used on the head.' The body was blood-spattered, and Mrs Millward's shoes were missing. There was no evidence of sexual molestation.

A male witness had come forward to tell that he had heard Vera Millward's last spine-chilling screams. There was a 'Help! Help! Help!' the last cry cut off abruptly and then just silence. As it was near the Infirmary, the witness thought it was a hospital patient having a nightmare. Mr Ridgeway remarked, 'The trouble with this whole area is that a scream in the night is not unusual.'

What impressed investigators was the fact that the murderer seemed to have taken a greater risk than ever before. The site of the murder was in fact very public, with more than eight hundred patients and staff in the surrounding hospital buildings. The whole area was floodlit and the car-parks nearby, which could well have been used by the killer, were in constant use by hospital visitors and by prostitutes and their clients.

Once more Mr Oldfield was to complain about the lack of public cooperation, suggesting that resentment of prostitutes' way of life could well be the reason. 'Why should we be concerned, they chose to lead this kind of life, so they must face the risks that go with it.' George Oldfield thus summed up the public's attitude.

Vera Evelyn Millward, who was also known on occasions as Anne Brown and Mary Barton, was last convicted as a prostitute in 1973. She was described by a neighbour as 'a quiet frail person who always seemed to be ill'. She weighed only eight stone five pounds. Her photograph reproduced in this book suggests a sick person who was racked by pain. Indeed Cy Burkett said that he thought when she left home on the fatal evening she was going to the hospital to get some pain killing drugs for stomach pains.

Vera Millward lived on the notorious Hulme Estate in Greenham Avenue in flats which have subsequently been modernised. A prostitute known as Janie, living in the same block of flats, said : 'I used to work the streets at the same time as Vera. Our beat was the Moss Lane, Denmark Road area.' Later, another good time girl, Jean, also operating in the same area, recalled : 'I did know Vera. She was only in it because she had kids to keep. She was car trade, Vera, although she had a special, I remember, someone who used to meet her regular in a big car.' The 'special', who drove a 1968 Mercedes, would signal his arrival by flashing his headlights outside Vera's flat. Detective Chief Superintendent Jack Ridgeway interviewed the man, who insisted their relationship was not sexual, although she would stay with him all night. 'They have known each other for five years,' said Mr Ridgeway. 'They would just talk. He would give her gifts of food and a small amount of money.'

Greater Manchester police again warned prostitutes of the risk they were running, and expressed the hope that they would operate in pairs and take down car numbers which might lead to the killer. Mr Ridgeway observed ruefully, 'There appears to be no noticeable reduction in their activities.'

Josephine Whitaker

The next victim was an innocent young girl, Josephine Whitaker, aged nineteen. She was found murdered face down in Savile Park, Halifax, a good class residential area some two hundred yards from her home. She had sustained severe head injuries and multiple injuries to the trunk.

The previous evening Joseephine had been to visit her grandparents to show them her new watch. As she was late to leave they suggested she should stay the night. Unhappily she decided to go home because she was worried about where to put her contact lenses. At home she used a special receptacle for them, a box indicating left and right lenses. She was a well-built and confident girl who was not afraid to return home in the dark.

The following day her brother David, aged thirteen, on his early morning paper round, saw police on the common where the body had been found, and recognised Josephine's shoe. He ran to his home in Vity Street, Halifax, where his parents, who thought Josephine was in bed asleep, discovered that she had not returned home the previous night.

It is most important to emphasise that, unlike so many of the victims in this case, Josephine was a teenager of completely blameless character.

At his Press conference on 16th April 1979, George Oldfield stated, 'The man is obviously mentally deranged, but he has now changed his pattern. The girl was perfectly respectable, in an open space and legitimately going about her business. We always felt he would strike again, but we are now faced with a new situation. We cannot stress how careful every woman must be. Unless we catch him, and the public must help us, he will go on and on. This was another particularly brutal attack on an innocent young woman who was most respectable.'

The plea for information was taken up again by the Coroner, Mr James Turnbull : 'Come forward now and tell the police what you know before there is another tragedy. I pray that whoever might be sheltering the person concerned, or who might have suspicions, will see the sense of that.'

Josephine Whitaker was killed in the Bell Hall district of Halifax. The area is one of open parkland overlooked by substantial Victorian residences built in yellow standstone, blackened by industrial pollution of a past age.

Josephine was a young clerk at the Head Office of the

Halifax Building Society. The area in which she was killed is rarely frequented by prostitutes. Her innocence and the tragic circumstances of her death determined the parents of Jayne MacDonald, another blameless victim, to break their grief-filled silence of two years. Irene and Wilfred Mac-Donald pleaded, 'If anyone has any suspicions, please come forward. How many more must die before people wake up and realise it could happen to someone they love.'

Wilfred MacDonald told how he would always remember his daughter Jayne leaving home on her last date. 'She was so sweet and clean and she bent down and kissed me goodbye. She was untouched and perfect, just like a flower,' he said. He would always remember the horror of identify-ing her : 'It was her hair, I can't get it out of my mind,' he said. 'It had looked so blonde and soft a few hours before, and now it was hard and caked with blood . . . I have been suffering from asthma ever since . . . I beg anyone who might be able to offer any shred of help which might lead to the Ripper's capture to remember the way I felt when I looked down upon my darling that morning. Let them try to imagine my hell and for God's sake let them not remain silent a second longer.'

Mrs MacDonald talked of her family's torment : 'No one can ever know what it is like when your child is murdered. I wept when I heard about Josephine Whitaker. For those they left behind there will never be peace again . . . A murder doesn't just end with the victim. It spreads hideous ripples throughout a family. In a way it kills them all.' Mrs MacDonald then went on to describe the effect of the murder on her other children. Jayne's younger sister had become moody and an older sister had had a near nervous breakdown. Her brother had become withdrawn.

Josephine Whitaker's memorial service was held at St Jude's parish church, Halifax, where the family attended services. Detectives mingled with some six hundred mourners. The service was conducted by the Vicar, the Reverend Michael Walker. He said, 'This tragedy has made many conscious of the devotion to duty of our police. This

6   81

service would be inadequate without my expressing the town's appreciation of the police and the town's prayers that their efforts might soon effect the murderer's arrest.'

Further sadness was inflicted on the MacDonald family with the death of Wilfred MacDonald in early October, 1979. Wilfred never recovered from the sight of his murdered daughter and developed nervous asthma and chronic bronchitis soon after the killing. He was never able to work again and it is probably no exaggeration to attribute his sad and premature death to the vicious slaying of his daughter.

Barbara Leach

It is with the appalling murder of Barbara Leach, a twenty-year-old student at Bradford University, that the sad catalogue of the present day Ripper's crimes is brought up to date (September 1979). Fears will continue to mount in the West Riding towns for as long as the Ripper remains at liberty. To date it is thought he has killed no less than twelve times, three times in Bradford, and, as we have seen, he has in addition made a number of vicious attacks on women which have not proved fatal. As the killer had promised on his chilling tape released by the police, he would strike again, maybe in September. In fact the killer struck shortly after midnight on the first day of the month.

The latest gruesome killing was discovered by a policeman at Back Ashgrove, a stone's throw from Bradford University. The victim, described as a lovely, friendly girl, with a golden future, is remembered as vivacious and an extrovert. Barbara, who came from Kettering, was battered to death and mutilated just two hundred yards from her flat in Horton. Her body was found covered by a remnant of carpet near dustbins in a back yard.

Barbara Leach shared a terraced house with four men and two other women, all students, a few streets away from the scene of the murder. Detective Chief Superintendent Peter Gilrain, heading the Bradford inquiry, said Miss Leach had been at the Manville Arms public house in Great Horton Road with her flat-mates until approximately 1 am on Sunday. They had all left together, but then Miss Leach decided to take an early-morning walk on her own.

Mr Gilrain said that for a woman to take a walk late at night on her own was a very foolish thing to do, bearing in mind that the killer had already claimed eleven victims. Mr Gilrain said, 'No woman in this part of the world should go out at that time. These are extremely brutal attacks, and he is now picking them at random, not just concentrating on prostitutes. In fact no woman in the north of England is safe until he is caught. The police can't protect every one of them.'

Back Ashgrove has been described as an area with a shifting immigrant population. It is basically well kept up and the mainly Victorian houses are divided into flats. It does not form part of the red light area.

On the night of her disappearance, Barbara Leach, a student in Social Science, was wearing trendy blue jeans with a cheeky badge reading 'best rump' affixed to the seat. Her blouse was long-sleeved and made of cheese cloth material. She wore red high-heeled boots covered by the jeans. She was also carrying a khaki haversack with shoulder strap.

It was not immediately apparent where the attack took place, but it could have been in Great Horton Road, which would have meant the murderer dragging the body to the yard in Back Ashgrove. Alternatively Barbara could have been attacked in Ash Road and carried or dragged down an alleyway to the yard behind 13, Ashgrove. Heavy rain, after the killing, might well have removed useful clues before the body was discovered.

Further warnings that women should not go about unaccompanied at night issued from the Bradford University Student Body and as Ripper hysteria mounted to new heights the Women's Rights Self Defence Organisation in Bradford intensified their campaign to be allowed to carry weapons.

Earlier in the year a Bradford woman had been arrested for carrying an anti-Ripper implement.

On 5th September 1979, the *Daily Star* revealed the 'agony that gripped three mums'. Apparently, in the fading light of evening, middle-aged mums scurry across waste ground to a police caravan to make amazing confessions: 'I think my son is the Yorkshire Ripper.' This has happened three times at the Mobile Incident Room in what is thought to be the Ripper's home town of Sunderland. Each suspect was carefully checked by the Ripper Squad and found to be guiltless.

After the twelfth murder the police were obviously coming under intense pressure. Police announced secret new plans to catch the Ripper. According to Detective Chief Superintendent Dick Holland these would take the form of extended cooperation between the regional crime squads based in Wakefield and Durham. Whether he was whistling to keep his spirits up or not, Mr Holland stated on BBC radio that an arrest could be just around the corner. He said, 'I've never worked on a murder where I know so much about the man I'm looking for.'

During a visit to Sunderland in July 1979, Mr George Oldfield had warned that an innocent person was being condemned to death because someone in the North was protecting the Yorkshire Ripper. This chilling prediction was tragically realised on 2nd September 1979. By now the amazing stamina evinced by Mr Oldfield during the long years of the inquiry had given out, and he was required to take a prolonged rest. Overall control of the investigation was then taken by Detective Chief Superintendent Jim Hobson, who dashed from the hospital where his wife was being treated for a fractured skull, having fallen downstairs, to a meeting with pathologist David Gee and Detective Chief Superintendent Jack Ridgeway of the Manchester force.

It would seem that a number of investigating officers have struck misfortune during the inquiry, Mr Hobson himself being a replacement for Chief Superintendent Dennis Hoban who died suddenly at an early stage in the inquiry.

CHAPTER SEVEN

Catch Me If You Can

Perhaps the most bizarre Press Conference in the annals of British crime detection was held at Wakefield on Tuesday, 26th June 1979. The conference was attended by top brass from the four police areas involved in the Ripper investigation: West Yorkshire, Northumbria, Lancashire and Manchester. Flanked by Detective Superintendent Holland (the head of the Ripper squad), Mr George Oldfield played a tape which he believed had been sent to him by the Ripper himself. Police and journalists listened in rapt attention to the tape-recorded voice. The Ripper's broadcast to the nation began:

I'm Jack, I see you are still having no luck catching me.

I have the greatest respect for you, George, but Lord, you are no nearer catching me now than four years ago when I started.

I reckon your boys are letting you down, George. The only time they came near to catching me was a few months back in Chapeltown when I was disturbed. Even then it was a uniform copper, not a detective.

I warned you in March that I'd strike again. Sorry it wasn't Bradford. I did promise you that, but I couldn't get there. I'm not quite sure where I will strike again, but it will be definitely some time this year, maybe September or October, even sooner if I get the chance. I'm not sure where – maybe Manchester. I like it there, there's plenty of them knocking about [a reference to prostitutes].

They never learn, do they George? I bet you've warned them, but they never listen.

At the rate I'm going I should be in the Guinness Book of Records. I think it's eleven up till now, isn't it?

Well I'll keep on going for a while yet. I can't see myself being nicked just yet. Even if you do get near I'll probably top myself first. Well, it's been nice chatting to you, George. Yours, Jack the Ripper. No good looking for fingerprints. You should know by now it's as clean as a whistle. See you soon. Bye.'

There then followed an extract from a pop song by Andrew Gold called 'Thank you for being a friend.'

A personal impression of the voice and delivery was that it was both muted and self-controlled. This would be quite compatible with the behaviour to be expected from a psychopath. The message sounded as though it had been read from a prepared text, and its sender may possibly have had a couple of drinks before recording it. It seemed too well formed to have come out spontaneously. There was little sign of hesitation and the message seemed quite compact. The voice sounded as though it could belong to a man in the twenty-five to forty age range.

At this stage it is impossible to establish with absolute certainty the genuineness of the tape. There remains a possibility that it may be no more than a cruel joke. However Mr Oldfield was obviously fairly confident that he was in possession of the genuine article. The handwriting on the envelope in which the tape was sent was the same as that in three other letters received by the police from the Ripper, one of which had been passed on by the Manchester office of the *Daily Mirror*. Each of these contained intimate details about the killings which police believe only the Ripper could know.

After the release of the recording, police took the Ripper tape on a tour of factories and working men's clubs in the West Yorkshire area and beyond, but to date they have not announced that any positive identifications of the voice have been confirmed.

I consulted Dr John Baldwin, Lecturer in Phonetics and Linguistics at University College, London, who told me that voice identification and matching is by no means a simple process. In fact, he said, there is no such thing as a voice print. Dr Baldwin advised on tape recordings in the Jeremy Thorpe case, and his evidence resulted in an acquittal in the case Regina v. Savage. Savage was accused of making black-mailing telephone calls. By examining tapes taken of the telephone calls Dr Baldwin was able to establish that they were not in fact made by Savage. Dr Baldwin pointed out that voice patterns are far too complex to allow for a process of mechanical sorting. The notion that taped speech samples can be processed by computer is apparently still in the realm of science fiction. This was confirmed by Mr George Stern, a senior statistician and computer expert, who described the less complex but still daunting problems associated with computer techniques for matching finger-prints: 'Particular problems arise in exact matching of blurred scene-of-the-crime prints; although human beings can't calculate as quickly as a computer they can be better at dealing with data which cannot be readily translated into numbers. A human expert may in fact be better at weighing up complex shapes and sounds and the inaccuracies and doubts involved.'

In view of this it is obvious that even if the police were to tape record all interviews with suspects, the process of attempting to marry up any of these with the Ripper original is both complex and time-consuming and subject to a signifi-cant degree of error.

Dr Baldwin pointed out that the place of birth of an individual is irrelevant in terms of speech characteristics, but that individual patterns of human expression are basically formed by the age of seven. These can, of course, be overlaid by environmental experiences, social pressures and other factors; people tend to adjust their speech to that which is acceptable among their contemporaries.

Speech, says Dr Baldwin, is composed of a whole number of variables, changing all the time. It is influenced by a range of emotions, tension, embarrassment, fear, the degree of sobriety, drugs, fatigue, general health, teeth, strokes etc. The larger the sample of speech available, the more accurate the assessment that can be made. It is noticeable that some people speak quite differently into a telephone or a tape recorder, which is a further complicating factor. If the Ripper tape is genuine the police have a valuable clue which could be the key to the case, but there was no absolute guarantee in July 1979 that the police would be able to make a quick arrest.

At the Press conference Mr Oldfield said that he believed that the man on the tape had been brought up in Sunderland but was now probably living in Yorkshire or Lancashire. Some dialect experts confirmed this analysis, but others apparently did not. Dr Peter Wright, Senior Lecturer in English, commenting on the tape, said : 'He does not come from Sunderland. Radio and TV are suggesting he speaks with a Sunderland accent, but this is not so. There is not a single thing on the tape that is particularly Sunderland. It is a Tyneside accent, placing him in Newcastle . . . He sounds a fairly young man, by the pitch of his voice in his early twenties. I would say he lived in the Newcastle area for the first twenty years of his life, picking up that area's distinctive sound.'

Unfortunately I am unable to help the reader resolve this semantic or tonal controversy, but would merely point out that Sunderland and Newcastle are within ten miles of one another and are situated in the general area where the Ripper is thought to originate.

On 29th June 1979, at a Press conference at Bishopsgarth, Wakefield, three days after allowing the tape to be broadcast, the police issued excerpts from a letter which they believed had been written by the Ripper. The letter was one of three received by the police which they considered to be genuine. The letters had been posted on 7th and 13th March

1978 and on 23rd March 1979. Each bore a Sunderland post-mark, which confirmed police suspicions that the killer had close links with the North East.

The letter of 13th March 1978 was in fact addressed to the 'Chief Editor of the Daily Mirror Publishing Office'. The first letter was addressed to 'Chief Constable George Old-field', whereas in the second, Mr Oldfield had been demoted to 'Assistant Chief Constable' – presumably the killer had become aware of Mr Oldfield's correct status during the year-long interval between letters.

Extracts from the letter dated 23rd March 1979 read as follows:

> Dear Officer, Sorry I haven't written, about a year to be exact, but I haven't been up North for quite a while. I wasn't kidding last time I wrote . . . That was last month, so I don't know when I will get back on the job but I know it wont be Chapeltown too bloody hot there maybe Bradford's Manningham. Might write again if up North.
> Jack the Ripper.
> P.S. Did you get the letter I sent to Daily Mirror in Manchester?

This taunting and chilling letter was received by Mr Oldfield thirteen days before the killing of Josephine Whitaker.

Mr Oldfield told the Press conference that the middle section of the letter had been deleted and he would not discuss details relating to the deletion. It is understood that the missing paragraph made a threat to kill again. It was also thought highly likely by journalists attending the Press conference that other correspondence from the Ripper prob-ably contained certain details of previous murders that only the police or the Ripper himself could know.

Police thought that the reference to up North was a red herring, an attempt to mislead them as to the killer's where-abouts. Mr Oldfield said, 'I believe he actually lives and works among us here in West Yorkshire. He definitely originates from the North East, but I feel he is down here. I believe this letter is genuine and hope people will study the handwriting carefully to see if they have ever seen it before.'

The letters were examined by a graphologist, Mrs Diane Simpson, who had previously demonstrated her skills on television. The art of graphology, which has long been used to assist European and American police where samples of handwriting have been available, has been slow to gain acceptance in this country. Mrs Simpson normally uses her skills as adviser to a staff recruitment agency. Diane Simpson described her technique of appraisal to Jill Armstrong of the *Yorkshire Post*: 'I look at the way people have chosen to alter their writing from the way they were originally taught; graphology is merely a question of cross checking,' she said.

It takes Mrs Simpson several hours to analyse a sample of handwriting. She would never normally work from a photocopy, which among graphologists is rather like looking at a print rather than an original oil painting. The first thing she does is to examine the back of the manuscript to see how much pressure has been exerted. She then looks at how much space has been left between words and letters and at the margins. She examines whether letters are joined together or printed and whether the lettering is simplified or neglected and slovenly. Mrs Simpson maintains that there is a difference between writing quickly and writing in a slovenly fashion. She then goes on to examine individual letters using a magnifying glass, looking to see how they are slanted and how the Is are dotted and the Ts crossed. She also looks out for crosses and hooks, a tiny hook at the end of a line can denote, she maintains, a stubborn streak, a reluctance to move on to the next line. The manner in which people cross their Ts can reveal whether they are angry or violent.

The Ripper letters were scrawled in biro on white lined paper. After careful study, Mrs Simpson advised the police that they did not appear to be the work of a crank and could well be from a man who had murdered ten women. She believed that the omission of certain words revealed the writer to be a Northerner from either Yorkshire or Lancashire. Mrs Simpson said : 'The writer is not pushing his own views or gloating over achievements the way cranks normally do; I deal with many crank letters in the course of my work, but these do not fall into this category.' Mrs Simpson then went on to say that she detected latent violence in the writer because of the way some of the words were stabbed into the paper. 'Even if the content were different, the hand shows a deep and dangerous force . . . Most people begin their writing strokes with a lot of pressure and ease off at the end of a stroke. That shows maturity. If a writer is very angry or intense about something he is putting on paper, he does exactly the opposite and at the same time his jaw will tense up . . . This angry reverse process is constant throughout the Ripper letters . . . This man really means business. I have no doubt he is quiet and a loner, but he is skating on thinner and thinner ice. There is tremendous attention to detail all the way through. I do not think he is particularly literate, but possibly reads a lot to learn facts.' Diane Simpson also thought that the Ripper would not be able to resist writing again.

At the earlier Press conference to launch the tape Mr Oldfield went on to comment on the Ripper's familiarity with areas of prostitution. 'He has an intimate knowledge of the red light districts in Yorkshire and Lancashire which a casual visitor could not have!' He was surely right in saying that with that kind of an accent the man, if he lived in Yorkshire, would stick out like a sore thumb.

One regional crime squad officer who had studied it said, 'This is the most incredible tape I have heard in my life. It's not boastful, almost like a personal chat between the Ripper and George Oldfield. It's as if he is saying "here I am, let's see if you are good enough to catch me".'

At her council house home, Mrs Maureen Long, who survived a brutal attack by the Ripper, listened to the tape recording on Pennine Radio. 'It frightened me,' she said. 'The way he was talking, slowly and deliberately, rang a bell in my mind. It made me angry, and if I had my way I would strangle him.' Since the attack near the Mecca night spot in Manningham Lane, Bradford, Mrs Long has been afraid to go out at night. She said, 'I have nightmares about him chasing me round the park, then killing me. I'm afraid to walk through subways on my own and even some TV programmes scare me now.'

In the days following the Ripper broadcast the police received some six thousand telephone calls. Presumably many of these were malicious and from people seeking to pay off old scores. However, Detective Superintendent Dick Holland expressed himself well satisfied with the public response. So much so that a telephone answering service dubbed 'Dial a Ripper' was installed whereby people could ring in to listen to the Ripper's tape-recorded voice. Unfortunately this proved so popular that police had to appeal to the numerous perverts and ghouls to get off the wire in order to keep the lines open. As a GPO official put it, 'The tape's as popular as the speaking clock.' A police spokesman said, 'We believe hundreds of people with a morbid curiosity to hear the Ripper's voice are blocking the lines.' One enraged detective was quoted as saying, 'We've been getting some calls from drunks thinking they're clever.'

Jonathan King, the pop impresario, had planned to produce six thousand copies of the recording as a commercial release through UK Records. However, after conversations with Mr Oldfield, who said that it was sad that anyone should want to capitalise out of the recording, restraint and a sense of good taste won the day and the project was dropped.

After the release of the Ripper tape recording Mr Oldfield was asked whether there had been any problems for the thousands of men who had been accused by their neighbours and relations. Mr Oldfield said, 'We are looking for a man who is a multiple murderer, who has himself caused a lot of anguish and grief to many people – the only man who has anything to fear is him.' At least the West Yorkshire Police can so far claim credit for not putting the wrong man on trial, which happened during the course of the London nude murders investigation and, in the Christie case, led to the wrongful conviction and hanging of Timothy Evans.

During a visit to Sunderland at the end of July 1979 Mr George Oldfield made another passionate appeal for assistance from the public. 'An innocent stranger is being condemned to a gruesome death because someone in the north is protecting the Yorkshire Ripper. Our only hope is to catch the Ripper before he can strike again.' Mr Oldfield returned to the theme that someone was sheltering the killer. 'It is as much in the killer's interest as the public's that whoever is shielding him should come forward. Obviously the Ripper is mentally sick and in need of treatment – the sooner he gets it the better.'

Throughout the summer of 1979 the police were active in following through the numerous leads provided by the public. They had no less than three hundred and fifty men on the case in West Yorkshire and Wearside alone. But, as Mr George Oldfield admitted in Sunderland : 'We have had a good response, but as yet no member of the public has been able to put the finger on the man we are looking for.'

One among the many leads the police received took them to Kellingley colliery near Pontefract. Kellingley employs over two thousand men and has a strong Geordie contingent among its workforce. Police said, 'There is no homing in on this particular area. There are many other inquiries going on in Yorkshire and the North-East. We are carrying out many checks on information we have received from the public. People must not feel that we are narrowing down the field. There are many leads taking us to many places and it is not at all clear which lead, if any, is taking us in the right direction.'

The tape recording in addition gave the police two other slender clues which were both followed up vigorously. The killer referred to being disturbed a few months previously in Chapeltown, Leeds. As a result of this revelation police sought a woman who had had an encounter with the Ripper at this time.

At the end of the tape the Ripper signed off with 'Hope

93

you like the catchy tune at the end, ha ha.' This was followed by a pop song, 'Thank you for being a friend'. Police sought information from stockists and pop music enthusiasts about any suspicious person acquiring the disc. Perhaps predictably, the search proved fruitless.

CHAPTER EIGHT

The Police Inquiry

Should the Yard be Called In?

In our society the police act not merely as custodians of our law and moral attitudes, but also by their actions frequently express these same values. It is quite natural, therefore, with a mass killer at large, that the police will seek to express the abhorrence of society and its determination to do something about it. Not unnaturally a vast police operation like the Ripper investigation will produce police activity which on occasion tends to be symbolic as distinct from purely functional.

Random and haphazard murder, where the killer is unknown to the victim, is extremely difficult to detect. Frequently the killer will give himself up or an informant will come forward to point a finger at the murderer. Often overcome with remorse and revulsion for his foul deeds the killer will commit suicide, in which case there is normally sufficient forensic evidence to link him with the crime and the police are able to close their files. The Thames tow path murders, or the London Nude Murders, as they were called in the popular newspapers, are a case in point.

There is an internationally accepted rule that, where a murder is known to have been committed, the police will not close the file until the murderer is apprehended. In fact only about fifty per cent of cases throughout the world are solved.

In his book *Murder Investigation*, Frederick Oughton sets out police practice as it is normally followed upon the discovery of a murder victim. First it is the responsibility of the officer who is called to the spot to ensure that the immediate area surrounding the body remains undisturbed. It is his responsibility to establish if the corpse is in the same position as when it was found. When people discover a dead body they often behave in an irrational or panicky way, for example dragging it from a place of concealment into the open or attempting to revive it by turning it over. They frequently forget just what they have in fact done. The officer called to the crime should therefore keep the first witness with him until he or she has been thoroughly investigated. It is also his responsibility to make a detailed note of atmosphere and general weather conditions at the time of the discovery of the body. Such notes may assist the specialist officer and the pathologist to establish the time of death or indeed how long the body has lain in the place of discovery. An example of how helpful this may be is where a murdered person has lain near a working quarry. In such a case it has been found possible, by measuring the thickness of quarry dust deposits, to tell how many days the body has been there, and that, because the murder had occurred before this period, the murdered person had been killed elsewhere.

The specialist investigating officer is next on the scene; he is normally a man of scientific bent and has close professional contact with the pathologist both before the inquest and during the inquiry. It is with the arrival of the investigating officer that fingerprinting, photography and forensics begin. There follows a minute investigation of the ground, floor or carpet, pieces of which may be cut out for microscopic examination.

Meanwhile the police surgeon will probably have arrived to give an estimate of the time of death based on the process of *rigor mortis*, taking into account considerations of temperature.

A careful note is taken of all stains of blood, saliva, seminal fluid, etc. Great importance is also attached to the directions of the folds and creases in the victim's clothing. Forty or fifty photographs are taken of the murder scene from different angles.

1. Willomena McCann *(Yorkshire Post)*

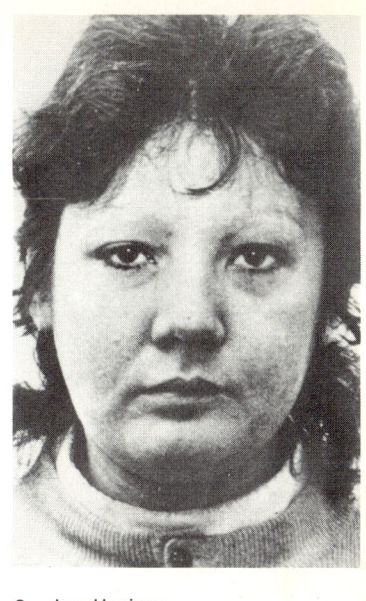

2. Joan Harrison
   (Lancashire Evening Post)

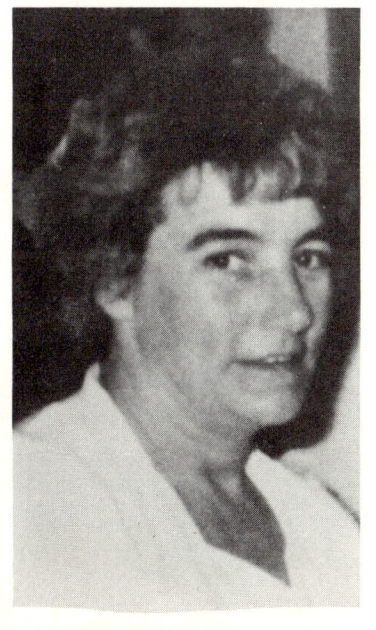

3. Emily Jackson *(Yorkshire Post)*

4. Irene Richardson *(Yorkshire Post)*

5. Patricia Atkinson *(Yorkshire Post)*

6. Jayne MacDonald *(Yorkshire Post)*

7. Jean Royle
(Manchester Evening News)

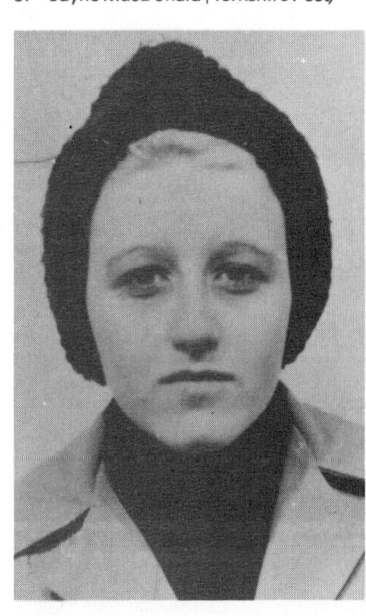

8. Yvonne Pearson *(Yorkshire Post)*

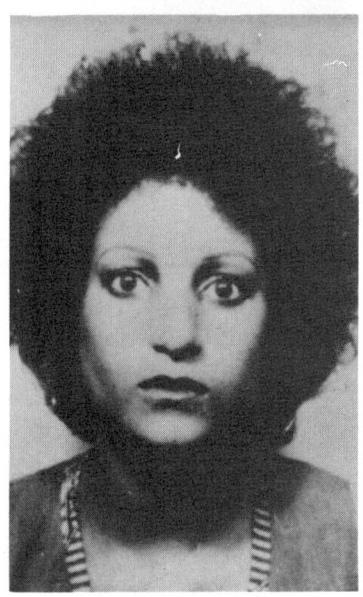

9. Helen Rytka *(Yorkshire Post)*

10. Vera Millward
(Manchester Evening News)

11. Josephine Whitaker

12. Barbara Leach *(Press Association)*

1. July 5, 1975
   Anna Rogulski
   Survived
2. August 15, 1975
   Olive Smelt
   Survived
3. October 29, 1975
   Willomena McCann
4. November 23, 1975
   Joan Harrison
5. January 21, 1976
   Emily Jackson
6. February 6, 1977
   Irene Richardson
7. April 24, 1977
   Pat Atkinson
8. June 25, 1977
   Jayne MacDonald
9. July 10, 1977
   Maureen Long
   Survived
10. October 10, 1977
    Jean Royle
11. December 14, 1977
    Marilyn Moore
    Survived
12. January 21, 1978
    Yvonne Pearson
13. January 31, 1978
    Helen Rytka
14. May 16, 1978
    Vera Millward
15. April 4, 1979
    Josephine Whitaker
16. September 2, 1979
    Barbara Leech

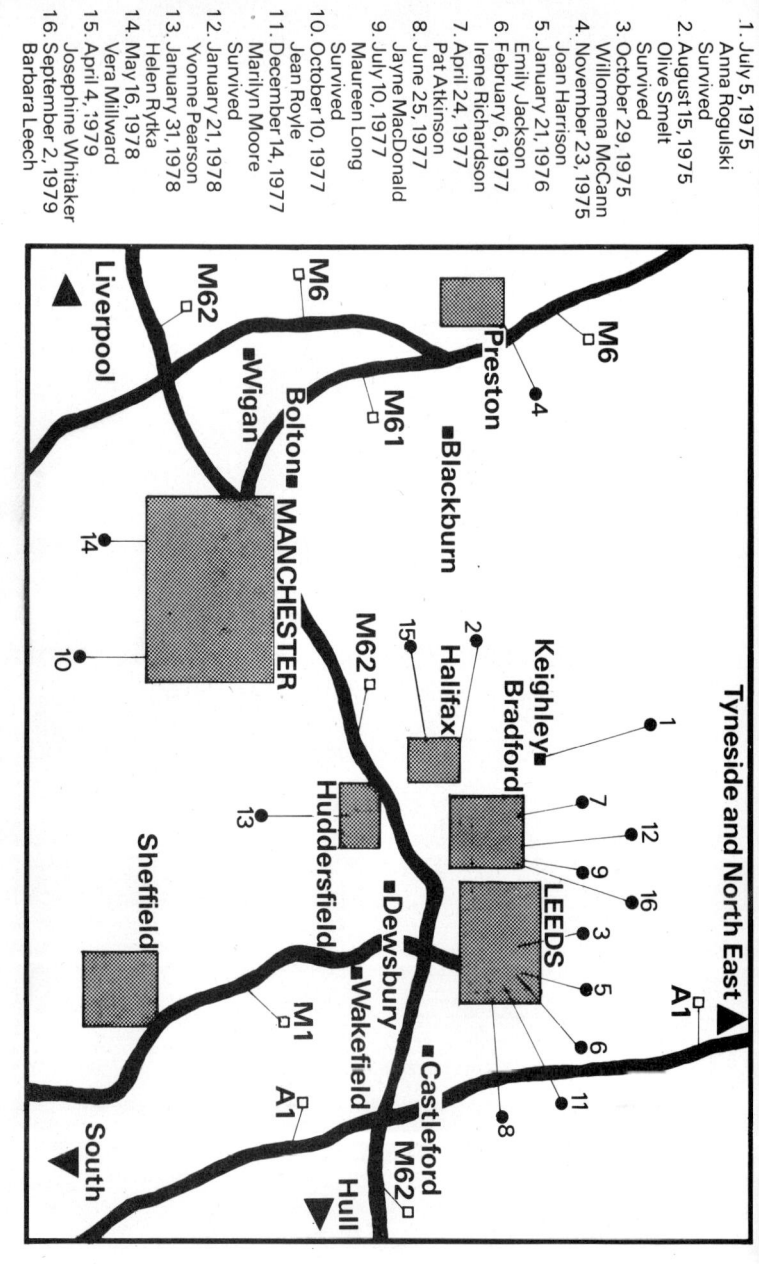

13. The photofit picture of the Ripper issued by the police in April 1979.
     (Press Association)

Dear Officer: March 23rd 79
        Sorry I hadn't written, about a year to be
recall, but I hadn't been up North for quite a while.
I wasn't kidding last time I wrote

                                                      That
was last month, so I don't know when I will
get back on the job but I know it won't be
Chapeltown too bloody hot there maybe
Bradford's Manningham. Might write again
if up North.
                    Jack the Ripper
P.S Did you get letter I sent to Daily Mirror
in Manchester.

14. A letter, received by George Oldfield, thought to have been written by the Ripper.
     The police have deleted part of the letter's content.

15. Peter Kurten, German mass murderer, convicted in 1931.

16. Neville Heath, convicted for the murder of two women in London, 1946. *(Press Association)*.

17. Marcel Petiot, convicted for twenty-four murders in France, 1946.

18. Assistant Chief Constable George Oldfield of the West Yorkshire Police playing the tape-recording believed to be from the Ripper, at a Press Conference in June 1979. Behind him is Detective Superintendent Dick Holland. *(Bradford Argos)*

19. Police in Chapeltown, Leeds, conducting a search after the murder of Jayne MacDonald in June 1977.

20. Police at Prince Phillip Playing Fields, Leeds, after the discovery of Wilma McCann's body in 1975.

When the operation is complete, items like clothes, hair, cigarette butts, broken glass, etc., are carefully marked, packed and sent for microscopic and chemical testing in the forensic laboratory. When finally all this is accomplished a reconstruction of the crime may be enacted.

Fingerprints have been accepted as evidence by the courts since 1909. It is thought that it may soon be possible to take them from the skin of a victim. Even in the case of a seemingly motiveless murder the placing of prints on record can serve a useful purpose, as in the case of Michael Dowdall (mentioned later) who was arrested for the murder of a Kilburn prostitute after an attack on another woman eleven months later. Dowdall's prints were found in the homes of both women. The Yorkshire Ripper himself seems to appreciate the significance of prints. In the tape recording addressed to George Oldfield, thought to have been sent by the Ripper, it is stated: 'No good looking for fingerprints. You should know by now it's as clean as a whistle.' Does this suggest that the Yorkshire killer protects his hands with gloves? It is very rare for a murderer to do so, also it would surely make him appear suspicious to his victims, particularly when he must also be carrying some heavy implements either in a bag or wrapped in paper or cloth. Glove prints can sometimes also provide a clue, leaving behind microscopic pieces of wool or material or actual prints where they have become saturated with blood or perspiration at the time of the murder.

In the case of the Ripper Mr George Oldfield has for some time been persuaded that the murder weapons the killer uses belong to his own trade. It had been noted that members of specific trades will often favour the tools of their trade as murder weapons. Every trade and profession has its own distinctive traces, generally in the form of dust, fibres or granules which can be readily identified under a microscope.

A blunt instrument can take many forms, such as a heavy torch or a tyre lever. A great deal depends on the nature of the instrument, for example, a claw hammer (possibly something like this was used by the Ripper) will do much more damage than a metal lever. Frederick Oughton, referring to blows on the head with a blunt instrument, states: 'A study of this type of murder suggests that after the first blow the victim will stagger or rock if standing, and if sitting will rise up in an involuntary agonised movement.' Such movement may frighten the murderer into dealing further blows of diminishing severity. A heavy blow may cause instantaneous death through severe shock. Shock occurs in a number of conditions, but is always due to a failure of the supply of blood to the vital function of the brain for one reason or another. Haemorrhage is a usual cause of shock; this occasions a general shortage in the supply of blood which immediately affects the brain. If the skull is merely fractured the victim may live if he or she receives immediate medical attention. If, on the other hand, the skull is fully caved in, death will be instantaneous. In the case of Joan Mary Harrison, the death certificate received from M. H. McCann, Coroner for Lancashire, after the inquest held on 25th November 1975 and 15th July 1976, gave the cause of death as:

(a) Haemorrhage and shock caused by
(b) Multiple injuries
Murder by Person or Persons Unknown.

The death certificates of the other victims in this case have not been available for my inspection but I would expect the stated cause of death to be similar in all cases.

In the 'normal' or more common type of murder the murderer leaves the weapon at the scene of the crime or discards it as he flees. Neville Heath (who is mentioned later) retained his weapon. It would appear that the Ripper, another abnormal murderer, also retains his weapons.

The science of blood grouping has been used for over seventy years and is now regarded as a precise science. This has an obvious importance in the detection of murder, when it is frequently possible to identify the blood grouping of both victim and murderer. As there are comparatively few blood groups this factor on its own could not provide absolute proof of guilt, but is of great assistance in many investigations. By using the advanced forensic aids of microscopy and spectroscopy more useful information may be gained. It has been found that the bodily origin of the blood can be most useful. It can be observed that blood taken from the nose, for example, differs from blood from the abdomen or lungs.

In cases where a blow has been inflicted on the head or where mutilation has occurred at or about the time of death, it is very rare for the murderer to be able to remove all traces of blood from his hands and other parts of his person, and from his clothing. Frederick Oughton states: 'Blows on the head will shatter small blood vessels in the scalp, causing blood to spray outwards over the murderer, and in the event of the skull being shattered, particles of brain matter and the protective fluid in which the organ rests will be found on clothing, in the hair and even deep inside the ears, as happened in one case, despite the murderer's precaution of taking a hot bath, cleaning his fingernails and washing his hair after burning his clothing. Blood of the same group as his victim was discovered in his ear.'

It is reasonable to assume from this that the Yorkshire Ripper must have been bloodstained after many of his crimes. It is also more than likely that forensic evidence linking him with the crimes will inevitably be discovered when he is apprehended.

The history of criminological investigation is rather like the history of warfare. Indeed, it is a kind of warfare eternally being waged between the criminal community on the one hand and the forces of law and order and the community at large on the other. There occurs a continual process of leap-frogging whereby the police make a technological advance and the criminal community compensates, catches up and attempts to overtake.

Detectives investigating the bloody crimes of Whitechapel Jack did not possess the elementary aids which are now to hand. These were committed in the days before fingerprinting and blood grouping had become accepted forensic aids and long before the existence of modern laboratory techniques in the fields of microscopy and spectrography.

Fingerprinting is an interesting example. This forensic aid, whilst still extremely important, is of diminishing value. Most criminals are aware of its significance although most murderers do not take it into account. However, it is possible to transpose fingerprints. Police investigating a murder case discovered a print on a window near the murder scene. This, it was found, belonged to a man who was dead before the murder had been committed! It was eventually discovered that the print had been taken from this man, who had been the victim of a gang killing, and planted at the scene of the murder by the conspirators.

Obviously, a fingerprint is only of use if it can be matched by one from a suspect, or one already on file. It is estimated that the police in Britain have more than two million prints on file awaiting matching.

It is reliably thought that one murder victim is embedded in the concrete pillar of a motorway. Clothing, murder weapons and other valuable evidence can similarly be disposed of in wet concrete. The phrase 'concrete overcoat' may have more than one meaning!

The Whitechapel slayer was able to flee bloodstained from the scenes of his crimes, skirting pools of light in the dimly lit streets of the East End and Westminster of his time. Even the sight of blood would not excite interest in a city where the Smithfield slaughterers went about their work at all hours and blood from the slaughter houses ran into the streets.

Now adequate street lighting exists in most towns, yet the macabre assassin of Yorkshire has other factors working in his favour. If his murder is well planned he will have a car strategically placed nearby, then all he has to do is to withdraw into the anonymity and relative safety of the family saloon car, taking his weapons with him. Obviously he does not use public transport. Imagine the Ripper with cuffs soaked in blood, clothing probably spattered with blood also, weapons in hand, waiting for the green bus at the bus stop in Chapeltown Road!

In the case of the Yorkshire Ripper the motor car is indispensable to the killer, not only for the getaway, but also for the opportunity it presents to attract women and to dispose of their bodies. By using a car the Ripper can also conceal his weapons from the women he picks up. Wilma McCann was probably picked up by the killer, because she had earlier been seen thumbing a lift. It is thought that the body of Emily Jackson may have been dumped from her own van, which the killer also used for his getaway, picking up his own car which was parked elsewhere. Irene Richardson was taken in a vehicle to Roundhay where her body was dumped. Marilyn Moore was attacked from behind as she was getting out of the Ripper's front passenger seat. Probably Jean Royle and Vera Millward were driven to the scenes of their death. The killer's opportunity is further enhanced by the motorway network which links all the northern towns involved in the inquiry and over which the police can only exercise a minimum of control without inconveniencing and antagonising members of the public. In any case the murderer would normally be home long before the murder is discovered. No better getaway system has so far been devised.

In their efforts to trace the killer the police have shown great interest in small boys' car registration number collections and those made by 'respectable women' offended by kerb crawlers. So far, however, the Ripper's car has not come to light. No doubt small boys and 'respectable women' are normally in bed by the time the Ripper sets out on his nocturnal forays.

The arrest of a cunning, mobile, random killer who is presumably not afflicted with remorse and where no accuser comes forward, has to depend on laborious and unglamorous detective work. It is police practice to work outwards from the scene of the murder; men are allotted a number of square yards to search with a fine tooth comb. As the inquiry proceeds, the area to be searched broadens. Similarly with interviews; these start with persons who discovered the corpse, relatives, friends, people in the street, all the time broadening out and becoming increasingly remote from the crime itself. As was mentioned in the case of Jayne MacDonald, of four hundred people known to be in Reginald Street on the night of the murder, which occurred well after midnight, the police were able to trace no fewer than three hundred and eighty; again in the case of Helen Rytka the police were able to trace over one hundred people who had been in Great Northern Street on the night of the murder. They accounted for all the cars in the street except three, and this despite the fact that inquiries did not start until days after the murder was committed.

Once these lines of inquiry have been completed, in the absence of forensic or material evidence, there is not really a great deal more the police can do except wait. In fact, in this case, so great has public interest now become, and so strong the determination of the police, that a system of surveillance has been introduced in certain towns with a view to capturing the killer should he attempt a further murder. It is here, one feels, that a certain element of symbolism has crept in to police work. It is obvious that a shrewd and cunning killer will quickly identify the surveillance and move further afield. The killer has after all already struck in six towns, and has obviously the means to travel anywhere in the United Kingdom. Again, spot checks on feeder roads to motorways could conceivably turn up the killer, and would certainly bring to light a number of other crimes, larceny and drunken driving in particular. It is, however, doubtful that the police would wish to jeopardise their delicate relations with the public by being seen as the cause of traffic snarl-ups and general inconvenience. It appears, therefore, that there is not much alternative to classic methods of detection. What the police really need is the kind of luck which occurred when a sharp-eyed copper noted a sly, backward glance, which led to the arrest and eventual conviction of the Black Panther, murderer of Lesley Whittle.

It may be worth noting that the archetypal example of a psychopathic killer given in Chapter One, Peter Kurten, was detected entirely by luck. A girl whom he had attempted to throttle wrote describing the incident, which she had not reported to the police, to a friend. The letter was misrouted and opened by a third party who took it to the police, who eventually succeeded in discovering the author!

The police operation which is centred on Wakefield is enormously expensive. To date (September 1979) it has cost in the region of three million pounds. Overtime earnings are high, and the joke circulating in the north is that as soon as overtime earnings begin to fall away a policeman goes out in search of a new victim. Any operation of this size and duration, involving something like 400–500 men full time, must generate a kind of ethos of its own. One imagines that it would be extremely difficult for the Chief Constable to curtail expense on the inquiry should he in fact wish to do so. Routines, disciplines, what is acceptable as overtime payment, have become a firmly estalished pattern. One young policewoman was quoted as saying, 'It becomes a way of life. On the other murders we have been working fourteen or fifteen hours a day without days off . . . Everything is dropped when a murder of this enormity is committed.'

I think it can be fairly stated that Detective Superintendent Richard Holland, Head of the Ripper Squad, and his boss Mr George Oldfield, Assistant Chief Constable, who has been in overall charge of the investigation, represent the older tradition within the police force. By this it is suggested that a younger generation of policemen are likely to be more detached and clinical in their approach, whereas men like George Oldfield have a strong and highly personal commitment to this kind of case. Mr Oldfield said in June 1979, 'It is a personal challenge. I suppose it is very much him against me.'

A week after the press conference at which the Ripper tape recording was first played in public, Mr Oldfield stated, 'I would like to talk to this man. And I feel he wants to talk to me. If he wants to phone me that would be fine . . . This has become something of a feud. He obviously wants to out-wit me but I won't pack it in until he's caught . . . He seems to like sending me things, and I suppose there is also the possibility that he might know me. I often sit for hours racking my brains to think if I might know him.'

Both Detective Superintendent Richard Holland and Assistant Chief Constable George Oldfield are men of end-less stamina, working fourteen hours a day on the case. For some years Mr Oldfield has been unable to complete the building of his greenhouse and when he lost his cucumbers in overnight frost, he told reporters: 'Cost me ten ruddy pence a seed.' Mr Oldfield, who has a Royal Navy back-ground, is now fifty-five years of age, and is eligible for retirement. But he says, 'I don't intend to give up until we have sorted this one out.' A heavy smoker, known to enjoy a glass of Scotch, he likes to relax with a gun on the grouse moor if he ever has the time.

An incident during the Ripper hunt demonstrates his devotion to his job. Driving home late at night, he spotted a man lifting some stone from a farm wall and promptly stopped to arrest him.

His colleague Superintendent Dick Holland, who at eighteen-and-a-half-stone plays prop forward in police rugby, also works round the clock. His meticulous approach to police work was illustrated in a murder case in 1977 when he was looking for a man who killed a boy scout. His only clue was a fibre drawn from a piece of carpet. Thirty-two miles of carpet had been sold. Holland accounted for it piece by piece, until it eventually led him to the killer.

It is fervently to be hoped that this deep personal commit-ment on the part of the pursuers, and their personalised style of investigation, will encourage further communi-cation from the killer himself. Perhaps it is not impossible that this factor, combined with an inflated ego continually being enlarged by press coverage, may eventually compel the killer to step forward in a blaze of publicity to meet his adversaries.

By early 1979 rumbling discontent at the lack of progress by the police began to be expressed in the Press. In June Nicola Tyrer asked in the London *Evening News*, 'Why won't they call in Scotland Yard? Many people feel that if the police were on the ball they would have caught him by now.' The recognised procedure is that Scotland Yard will only intervene in a case at the request of the Chief Constable of the relevant police authority. In this investigation at least three authorities would be directly involved in such a request. Quite obviously men with such professional dedication and pride in their own forces as George Oldfield would be reluctant to advise their Chief Constables to request assistance from the Yard. For his part the Chief Constable of the West Yorkshire police, Mr Ronald Gregory, would be against any such move. Mr Gregory stated, 'There is no way that I would call in Scotland Yard in this case. That is not to decry the Metropolitan Police in any way because they are a very good force indeed. But a force the size of West Yorkshire [5,000 men] has as much and possibly more experience than Scotland Yard officers would have if they came to help.'

When I mentioned the notion of bringing in the Met to Detective Superintendent Dick Holland, Head of the Ripper Squad, he said it was a thoroughly insulting suggestion. On the other hand, Chief Constable Albert Laugharne, head of the Lancashire force, expressed a somewhat different view. He told a police conference, 'Aid sought by a small force from a larger is a situation which, despite increasing major incidents, may still be done somewhat reluctantly. It is done less often than it ought ideally to be, if the Chief Constable feels that he thereby throws doubts on his self-sufficiency.'

My own impression derived from conversations with Yard officers is that the Metropolitan Police are not in any case anxious to become involved.

In April 1979 Geoffrey Mather of the *Daily Express* asked Assistant Chief Constable George Oldfield whether it had been suggested that Scotland Yard's murder squad be called in to help. 'It has any number of times,' he answered, 'but all the Yard would send would be a Chief Superintendent and a Sergeant – two men who would not know the area and would be worse off than we are.' George Oldfield also reacted in a prickly manner when asked on another occasion whether he could do with some assistance from the Yard. 'They haven't caught theirs yet,' he said, a reference no doubt to the Whitechapel murders of the eighteen eighties.

Indeed there seem to be no compelling reasons why the Yard should be called in; no reason to believe in fact that they would achieve any greater degree of success. The large Northern police forces which have become involved have not stinted resources on the case. In fact some would argue that the allocation of manpower and resources has been if anything profligate. According to my researches Mr Oldfield showed some resentment when the point was put to him. He said he was investigating [at that time] eleven murders and four attempted murders, and the possibility of further murders being committed fully justified the maximum use of manpower and expense, and that neither effort nor wit should be spared in an effort to bring the criminal to book.

The best professional advice is readily available. Throughout the inquiry forensic work had been handled by regionally based Home Office pathologists and a welter of psychiatric advice has been received from eminent psychiatrists.

If a new team was introduced into the inquiry at this stage it would face the formidable task of getting to grips with four years of investigative work. As Nicola Tyrer discovered on a visit to the central incidents room at Millgarth police station, it was bulging with paperwork. All information given to the police is filed, indexed and cross-referenced. There is a section, for example, on unidentified people containing such categories as 'beards', 'glaring eyes', 'speech defects' and 'boasters'. All that would happen if fresh investigating officers were brought in would be that they would become submerged in a sea of paperwork. It is a recognised difficulty of police work that the longer an inquiry takes the more difficult it is to backtrack over the evidence.

In September 1979, after the chilling prediction uttered on the tape to George Oldfield was finally realised, Mr Ronald Gregory, Chief Constable of West Yorkshire, spoke to the Press. He said, 'The morale of the men is high because they are confident that eventually they will get this man. It's an extremely difficult inquiry because this man has the initiative to strike at any time, anywhere, when there are few or no people about. It would need thousands of police officers to cover the area of West Yorkshire that we would need to do to try and catch him; so we have to try to catch him by other means. At no time has there been any question of the men's morale being low.' Mr Gregory, however, did take a swipe at the *Daily Express*. He said, 'The report in the *Daily Express* that the Home Secretary is to set up a squad of senior officers to lead the hunt is false. I know nothing of it; the Home Office know nothing of it. I'm amazed that this newspaper, who are normally helpful to murder investigations, should embark upon this form of speculative and provocative journalism. It can do nothing but harm to the inquiry, and can seriously undermine the morale of the investigating officers . . . I deplore this irresponsible imputation against the professional abilities of my officers.'

In the late summer of 1979 certain changes, albeit of a temporary nature, had become necessary in the top leadership of the inquiry. By October it had become apparent that George Oldfield was unable to undertake a speedy resumption of his responsibilities after a serious illness during the summer. It fell to Mr Ronald Gregory, Chief Constable of West Yorkshire, assisted by Detective Chief Superintendent Hobson, to inaugurate a novel strategy in the continuing dragnet operation to find the Ripper.

Mr Gregory convened a press conference in Leeds at which he stated : 'There has never been an inquiry on this scale in the annals of police history.' He then went on to announce details of 'Project R', a massive advertising campaign aimed at catching the Ripper, the cost of which would be one million pounds, but only about £20,000 of which would be borne by the police authority. Television, radio, newspapers and advertising companies would all be giving their services free. 'Never before,' said Mr Gregory, 'has this sort of huge publicity campaign been attempted, not even in America . . . This is not a circus . . . We are out to catch the worst killer in British criminal history. We have to be careful,' he added, 'we do not advertise the Ripper like some breakfast food or beverage, but only in this way can we reach every member of the public. I make no apology for intruding into the privacy of everyone in this country. We want to shake the public conscience and get everyone to help us . . . Obviously we could be accused of sensationalism. I hope not. What we are looking for is a dramatic impact.'

During the press conference Mr Gregory also stated, perhaps rather ominously, that: 'This paranoic who hates women is not going to be caught by Sherlock Holmes detection.' He seemed to be confirming the suspicion that despite an enormous accumulation of 'evidence' the Ripper would be unlikely to be ensnared by conventional methods of detection. Mr Gregory stated: 'it is a friend, a neighbour or relative who will eventually lead us to him.'

The million-pound advertising campaign was masterminded by Leeds advertising executive Mr Graham Poulter in cooperation with West Yorkshire Community Affairs Officer, Superintendent Peter Silvester. The Graham Poulter Group made an effective donation of £40,000 by foregoing payment on creative work and executive time. Headlines designed by the Group for display on poster sites, buses, and at supermarket checkout points included: 'Ignore the Ripper and he'll go away . . . to kill again. The man next to you may have killed 12 women. The Ripper would like you to ignore this.'

In addition, a gruesome four-page 'Catch the Ripper' newspaper was issued to be delivered by eight and a half thousand newsagents to a million homes between Stoke on

Trent and Berwick on Tweed. Six and a half thousand sites carrying sixteen sheet posters (10′ × 6′8″ of advertising space) were offered free throughout the country for a month. The BBC produced a Ripper item and independent radio broadcast recordings of the Ripper's voice.

It is dispiriting to record that a month after Project R was launched and despite the enormous public response generated by it, the Ripper had not been apprehended. Writing in *The Observer* on the fourth anniversary of the murder of Wilma McCann, Denise Winn stated that the police fear their chances of catching the Ripper 'are now diminishing rather than increasing. Their nightmare is that unless he strikes again, he may remain free for the rest of his days'.

The public response to Project R was quite remarkable. Not only were the specially reserved telephone lines jammed, but the emergency 999 call system also became overloaded. No doubt the assessment and investigation of all the information given represents a continuing and very heavy commitment of police effort and resources.

CHAPTER NINE

Gazing into the Crystal Ball

A sensational series of killings always attracts a great deal of public attention which becomes focussed on a variety of community problems and offers a political platform for social activists. The Ripper case is no exception. Prominent in these ranks have been members of the women's movements, who quite understandably relate the vicious attacks on women to the general problem of violence against women in society.

Mr George Oldfield has attracted a considerable amount of flak from this source. In an understandable effort to overcome public apathy he has been at pains to stress the innocence of two of the victims, Jayne MacDonald and Josephine Whitaker. According to the magazine, *Spare Rib*, 'The Ripper killings are, as feminists in Leeds point out, only at the extreme end of the scale of violence women face every day. from being touched up in the street at the "frivolous" end of it, through to battery and rape.' In the flood of Ripper publicity, this connection is rarely if ever, made. The article by Eileen Fairweather entitled 'Leeds Curfew on Men' goes on to argue that by focussing on the 'virtue' of the victims, attention is drawn away from who is to blame, i.e. men, not women.

When Josephine Whitaker had been murdered, George Oldfield had said, 'It would look as if in this case, as with Miss MacDonald, he [the Ripper] made a mistake – Miss Whitaker, a building society clerk, was a perfectly respectable girl.' Ms Fairweather resented the implication that the murdered women had somehow 'asked' for it. As the Leeds

Other Paper put it, this exactly corresponds with the tone of posters Bradford police had on their vans : 'The next one could be innocent'.

These lessons were not lost on the young ladies of Leeds Girls High School, who began training in unarmed combat to counter the Ripper menace. A sixteen-week course organised by Mr Eddie McGee, who had taught hundreds of soldiers and policemen self-defence, was offered to the girls. Mr McGee said, 'The girls are now trained to go through an automatic check-list while they're being "attacked" by a class mate. They note the smell, size, height, shape and clothes of the attacker. It helps to steady their adrenalin while they prepare themselves for defensive measures and it will help the police afterwards.' Just how the girls were meant to do all this while being attacked from behind by an assassin with a hammer Eddie McGee did not make clear.

Magda, of the Leeds Rape Crisis Centre, did not consider the Ripper had killed the non-prostitute women 'by mistake': 'When you hate women as much as he must, *any* woman will do. Prostitutes are simply more vulnerable targets.' She also felt that the enormous publicity given to the women's prostitution had probably hindered catching the Ripper. 'Hundreds of people have phoned with information about the women who weren't prostitutes, but the police themselves say they have had very few offers of information about the other women. The attitude seems to be that prostitutes just don't matter.'

As part of a week of action, 'Women against Violence against Women' organised a questionnaire which revealed that over seventy per cent of women answering the questionnaire had been 'kerb-crawled' or 'flashed'.

Inevitably in an inquiry of this sort a lot of cranks, loonies and odd-balls begin to crawl out of the woodwork. The Ripper case also has attracted its fair share of hypnotists, soothsayers and clairvoyants. Simon Alexander, for example, expressed his intention of visiting the scenes of the Ripper's crimes to pick up 'vibrations'. These vibrations were to lead him to the Ripper's front door, but unhappily after he had spent several hours with the Leeds police the vibrations yielded little of value. In June 1977 Alfred Cartwright, a clairvoyant and medical herbalist for forty-two years, offered Leeds police a description of the killer. Yorkshire clairvoyant Stanley King has told how he saw the Ripper in a dream in a small village high up in the Pennines. His vision was so strong, he stated, that he felt impelled to give the police a description of the place. Mr King also suggested that the Ripper was connected with the motor trade.

On 1st July 1979 the *Sunday People* announced on its front page that famous clairvoyant Doris Stokes had 'seen' the face of the Ripper. Doris Stokes stepped confidently into the mystic arena fresh from triumphs in California where she had been assisting the police. Apparently she had been able to name the victim, his wife and a detective in the case twenty-four hours before the body was found! According to Mrs Stokes the Ripper 'is about five feet eight inches tall and in his mid-twenties to thirties with dark hair and a scar below his left eye which twitches when he gets agitated'.

Mrs Stokes, who had studied the tape recording, believed that the killer's mother was called Polly or Molly. 'I got through to the killer's mother,' said Mrs Stokes, 'she told me he was married but his wife had left him . . . I get the feeling that he is a sort of genius turned the other way.' And she added, 'Johnny, Ronnie, or whatever your name is, you're going to get caught. You may as well give yourself up.'

Called upon to comment, Northumbria's Assistant Chief Constable, Mr Brian Johnson, said, 'Clairvoyants over the years have given their services to the police and we shall certainly investigate what she has to say.' Mr Johnson undertook to investigate all the street names given by Mrs Stokes. Unfortunately her description of the Ripper was not sufficiently precise to avoid the possibility of wrongful suspicion. Doris had said that Johnny or Ronnie's address included the word Berwick or Bewick. Angry denials were shortly to issue from long-distance lorry driver Ronnie

Metcalf of Berwick Avenue, Downhill, Sunderland. 'It's not me, so just lay off,' he said in a Wearside accent. 'I seem to fit the bill almost exactly. At first I didn't mind having my leg pulled, but really this is no laughing matter. There are bound to be people who take this clairvoyant stuff seriously and who will be pointing their finger at me.'

Unemployed builder's labourer Hector Hill encountered similar misfortune. He said in his flat in Sunderland that for several days before two detectives called, people had been knocking on his door and shouting through his letter-box. 'People who had heard the Ripper tape decided to get me pulled into the inquiry for some michievous reason,' said Hector. He also told reporters that when the policemen called they asked him to write a letter as if he were applying for a job. Presumably their request was in order to enable them to make a comparison with the Ripper's handwriting.

Another leading clairvoyant who became involved in the case was a Mrs Tracey, who derived her inspiration from a study of the Ripper's handwriting on the letters received by Mr Oldfield. Her view was that the killer was basically a gentle person with a 'deep psychological mother rejection'.

To conclude this summary of the paranormal aspects of the case reference might perhaps be made to the 'moon madness' theory. Certain research emanating from behind the Iron Curtain suggests that there could be a relationship between the orbital effect of the moon and psychopathic behaviour. The theory has been taken up by Dr Lieber of Miami University and entitled the 'Lunar Effect'. Apparently the full or new moon is likely to be the most explosive time. Dr Lieber thinks that under these conditions the moon creates a gravity pull on Earth sufficient to send the un-balanced psychopath over the edge. Perhaps this is not as extraordinary as it sounds when one recalls that the föhn wind (a persistent Alpine wind which creates nervous anxiety) is often cited as a mitigating circumstance in Swiss murder cases. However, a matching of the murder dates with the phases of the moon does not reveal any discernible correlation.

On 26th July 1979 Manchester astrologer Reginal du Marius predicted that 'the Ripper will strike tomorrow'. Fortunately, unless an unknown victim awaits discovery, the 27th July was not marked by a further outrage. Mr du Marius based his erroneous calculation on the fact that 'the Ripper strikes when the moon is positioned in an orbital course of 22 degrees'. Mr du Marius, a professional astrologer for six years, said, 'I've also deduced that the Ripper was born at 9.30 pm on September 15th 1946.'

In his distinguished compendium of Ripperology *The Complete Jack the Ripper*, Donald Rumbelow describes how the Victorian police took photographs of the eyes of the Whitechapel murder victims. The theory was that the retina would retain the final image of the assailant which could be reproduced by the photographic process. So far as I know this is one of the few lines of inquiry which have not been tried in this case. Incidentally, the last evidence of this superstition occurred in 1928 when P.C. Gutteridge was shot through the eyes by two villains, Browne and Kennedy.

It was not until July 1979 that clairvoyancy consultant Mrs Nella Jones brought her expertise to bear on the Ripper case. Earlier in the year she had been assisting Japanese police in a bid to help them with a few unresolved crimes. Mrs Jones, a life-long clairvoyant, claimed, 'I have been inside the mind of the Ripper – I knew just what he was thinking.' Nella Jones became 'locked into the mind of the Ripper' whilst sitting in her Kentish home with a South London policewoman. They were having a cosy chat at the time, and then the atmosphere in the room became almost unbearable. 'I just remember the policewoman turning pale and jumping out of her chair to run out of the room. I was actually with the Ripper in Yorkshire,' said Nella. The policewoman, who was born in Yorkshire, was able to identify the location of the encounter from Nella's description, placing it in Filey on the Scarborough Road. Nella Jones recalls that the Ripper was 'carrying an army haversack – the sort men use to take their sandwiches to work – over his left shoulder. And he wears a thick leather belt around his waist. He was definitely mentally sick, with an uncontrollable urge to kill. He feels he has to justify this urge by choosing a certain type of woman as his victim, as if he were some instrument of good in the world, handing out justice. But he is not going to stop there, he is going to kill again if he is not caught soon, only I feel that this time it could be a young boy of fifteen or sixteen.'

Nella Jones' description of the Ripper is similar in some ways to that provided by Doris Stokes. Five feet seven inches or five feet eight inches tall, at thirty-six he would seem to be a little older, and the scar in a different place: 'A fine white line like a scar running from his nose into his upper lip.' Mrs Jones did not observe the Ripper's agitated twitch.

In common with other clairvoyants, Nella found the Ripper to be 'a very clever man, and that is the most important thing about him. I don't mean he could sit down and write a book, but the knowledge he has in his head is fantastic. He could have been a genius gone wrong. I don't think he has ever married, but I believe his mother is dead and that his father was a cripple . . . I have the feeling he was taken away from his mother when he was ten or eleven years old.'

CHAPTER TEN

Psychopath or Sadist: Categorising the Ripper

Is the Ripper a psychopath? Is he a sadist? Is he a 'violent sex offender'? We will attempt to examine these different categories to see whether we are able to get a little closer to the Ripper.

In the first place, what is psychopathy? 'We are satisfied we are looking for a psychopath. He is brutal, calm and cunning, but he is driven by some terrible urge: when it overcomes him he flips.' (George Oldfield.)

'The Ripper is likely to have a grossly abnormal psychopathic personality whose mission in life is to achieve a particular goal, however subhuman it might be.' (Professor Trevor Gibbens, forensic psychiatrist.)

Both policemen and psychiatrists are persuaded that the Ripper is a psychopath. Other psychiatrists believe that he is impotent and that his desire for sexual gratification has turned into a bloodlust. Another suggestion is that he has a pathological hatred of prostitutes. Perhaps his mother was a prostitute; perhaps he contracted VD from a prostitute; or perhaps he views prostitutes as the root cause of all evil in society and is waging a campaign to purge the community of prostitution – 'a hygienic cleaning-up operation', as one psychiatrist put it.

Psychopathy might be one of the keys to understanding the Ripper's acts, as these authorities have suggested. But what is a psychopath? This term, like 'schizophrenia', is often misused. Professionals and laymen alike tend to apply it to behaviour they cannot otherwise explain. Only recently have psychiatrists begun to agree on a description of psychopathy, quite apart from its definition, diagnosis, or possible treatment; some authorities deny its existence altogether.

A common misunderstanding is to equate psychopathy with criminal behaviour or with various kinds of sexual aberration. Psychopathy is sometimes held to be the cause of most, if not all, crimes; but in fact only an insignificant minority of criminals have been diagnosed as psychopathic. The term 'psychopath' describes a particular kind of personality and not a type of criminal. Indeed, many psychopaths do not commit crimes at all.

The standard legal definition of psychopath in the United Kingdom (Mental Health Act 1959) says it is 'a persistent disorder or disability of the mind . . . which results in abnormally aggressive or seriously irresponsible conduct . . . and requires or is susceptible to medical treatment.' Psychiatrists are unhappy with this definition because it is imprecise and merely equates psychopathy with anti-social conduct.

In view of this, what is it that distinguishes a psychopath from other people? Professor Hervey Cleckley suggests the following points: 'Superficial charm and good intelligence, absence of signs of irrational thinking, absence of nervousness; unreliability, untruthfulness and insincerity; lack of remorse or shame, inadequately motivated anti-social behaviour; poor judgement and failure to learn by experience; pathological egocentricity and incapacity for love . . . specific loss of insight; suicide rarely carried out; sex life impersonal, trivial, and poorly integrated; failure to follow any life plan.'

Similarly William and Joan McCord describe the typical psychopath as being asocial, driven by primitive desires, highly impulsive, aggressive, feeling little guilt, and with a warped capacity for love.

These distinct features of psychopathic personalities have been noted by observation of their behaviour and by psychological tests. But, in addition, these tests on people already diagnosed as psychopaths have discovered physiological differences between them and other people.

A person's physical reactions to fear, excitement, or threat of punishment can be measured by monitoring the action of the nervous system. Tests performed on psychopaths have shown that their bodies react less to external stimuli than those of 'normal' people, and that their brainwave activity is sometimes more like a child's. It is possible that some psychopaths have defective or immature nervous systems or brain mechanisms. Their reactions are abnormal, but this does not mean that they are intellectually deficient or childish.

These findings suggest that psychopaths are emotionally 'flat' and do not respond to situations which would, in others, produce feelings of excitement, anxiety or fear. Nor do they experience the more social emotions of shame, guilt, remorse, or embarrassment which are learned in early childhood and go to make up the developed conscience. Because these emotions develop in childhood, it is obvious that upbringing and early experience will affect the adult's 'conscience'. Although diagnosed psychopaths show some physiological differences, these of themselves are not necessarily enough to account for their abnormal personalities.

Studies of the family backgrounds of psychopaths show that a very high proportion come from broken or emotionally improverished homes, often with alcoholic, brutal, or anti-social fathers and weak, absent, or rejecting mothers. William and Joan McCord argue that 'brain damage alone does not result in the distinctive characteristics of the psychopath: guiltlessness and lovelessness'. They suggest psychopathy may be caused by either severe rejection by one or both parents, or mild rejection combined with some abnormality of the brain or nervous system, or mild rejection combined with other influences such as a psychopathic father, punitive discipline and the absence of supervision.

More recent research is beginning to identify two distinct types of psychopath: simple and hostile. Hostile psychopaths tend to come from very disturbed family backgrounds, to commit crimes against the person such as assault, rape and homicide, to be impulsive and unpredictable, to lack anxiety, and to be incapable of forming any emotional attachments, appreciating the feelings of others, or anticipating the consequences of their own behaviour. Simple psychopaths, on the other hand, are less aggressive and tend to commit property crimes such as theft and fraud.

The Ripper certainly seems to display a lack of remorse and guilt, as well as being aggressive, unfeeling, egocentric, and perhaps impulsive. He may well be emotionally rather flat, even cold and callous, needing massive doses of stimulation from his environment to produce the same level of arousal, excitement, or even pleasurable fear that the rest of us get from normal sexual encounters, social gatherings, or even reading ghost stories. Significantly, one study found that twice as many hostile as simple psychopaths had done some military service. Perhaps brutal murder and assault is the only way the Ripper can attain some acceptable level of excitement. This excitement would be enhanced by the subsequent publicity and police search, and it is interesting to note the way in which he seems to have deliberately drawn attention to himself, needlessly increasing the risk of capture. Commentating on the tape, Dr Stephen Shaw, consulting psychiatrist at Wakefield, said, 'It seems this fellow is literally taunting the police. He is saying, "I can do no wrong. You haven't caught me on at least eleven occasions. Here is my actual voice. See what you can do now." This is typical of some psychopath seeking attention. One of the features of a psychopath is that he has an opinion of himself as being superior and better than anyone else. He believes he doesn't make mistakes, and if he does, he blames someone else.'

Psychopaths may not necessarily appear particularly cold or callous. They often seem at first to be intelligent and charming, with a sense of humour, and quite capable of showing all the outward signs of love and affection. They may even express conventional feelings of shock and horror when reading of their own crimes in the newspapers. But all this is a mask they have learned to assume. Neville Heath is a good example of a hostile psychopath and sadistic killer who managed to maintain this veneer of charm and normality.

In the case of the Yorkshire Ripper the murders are apparently sadistic. But psychopathy and sadism do not necessarily go together. Sadism (or sadomasochism) appears to be more common than is generally realised. Sadistic perversions have frequently appeared in literature: for example, the Marquis de Sade's novels and Sacher-Masoch's novel *Venus in Furs*. Swinburne's poetry too has a distinctive sadistic flavour:

> Ah that my lips were tuneless lips, but pressed
> To the bruised blossom of thy scourged white breast!
> Ah that my mouth for Muses' milk were fed
> On the sweet blood thy sweet small wounds had bled!
> That with my tongue I felt them, and could taste
> The faint flakes from thy bosom to thy waist!
> That I could drink thy veins as wine, and eat
> Thy breasts like honey!

> ... and pain made perfect in thy lips
> For my sake when I hurt thee; O that I
> Durst crush thee out of life with love, and die,
> Die of thy pain and my delight ...

In normal heterosexual relations the borderline between pleasure and pain may be very finely drawn. 'Love bites', for example, have been interpreted as a manifestation of vampirism, a recognised sub-type of sadism. Indeed the outstanding success of Bram Stoker's *Dracula* and its various derivatives points to a widespread, if repressed, interest in this form of sadism, and the eagerness with which accounts of brutalities in Hitler's Germany or Amin's Uganda are received may indicate some lurking sadistic tendencies in otherwise normal people. One might say the same of books about the Ripper.

Like psychopathy, sadism is a much misused word; it is often used to cover any and every act of cruelty and aggression. Strictly speaking it means the obtaining of sexual pleasure by the infliction of pain.

Dr Clifford Allen writes: 'The sadist is not universally dangerous. His aggressive emotion replaces affection in others; he maims and kills only those who, if he were normal, he would love. He is unable to express himself except in cruelty. In addition he is impotent in many cases, but if he does attain potency it is only by fantasy, or the reality, of the infliction of pain.'

The causes of sadism remain obscure. It is often associated with its apparent opposite, masochism, the obtaining of sexual pleasure from being hurt or humiliated. Some psychoanalysts think, with Freud, that man is born with a 'death instinct' which makes him wish to destroy himself and that masochism is derived directly from this. If this death instinct is directed outwards on to other people it becomes sadism.

Other psychoanalysts think that man is inherently aggressive and that all children are born in a 'state of hate', wishing only to attack and destroy everything, especially the mother's breasts: but if the child develops normally this hatred and aggression is transmuted into love. However, if the mother is hostile or indifferent this infantile sadism may carry through into adult life. This theory is supported by the fact that mutilations in the typical sadistic murder are centred on the genital region, abdomen, and breasts. Often the breasts will be cut off.

It is clear that sadism occurs where emotions of sex and aggression fuse into one. Normally there are strong inhibitions against the display of either sexual or aggressive impulses, but sadism, in common with many sexual perversions, contains a strong, compulsive, obsessive element. In other words, the sadist suffers from a persistent and overwhelming urge to realise his sadistic fantasies in real life.

Only after this has been done does he find any relief, albeit temporary, from tension.

The sadist who is also a psychopath is especially dangerous since the psychopath already has far fewer controls over his behaviour than other people. In addition, alcohol or drugs may act to remove the usual inhibitions on behaviour and bring to the surface latent sexual aberrations in otherwise normal people. A drunk sadistic psychopath can be very dangerous indeed.

The most extreme manifestation of sadism is the 'lust murder', a deliberate premeditated murder for sexual pleasure. Unlike more normal murders it is not inspired by anger or jealousy or despair or a desire for gain or revenge. According to Dr Allen it is characterised by: 'Periodic outbreaks due . . . to the patient's compulsion . . . nearly always cutting or stabbing, particularly of the breasts or genitalia, frequently with sucking, licking, or mouthing of the wounds, sometimes with biting of the skin. In some cases there is a desire to drink the blood and eat the flesh. No matter how revolting, the behaviour is pleasurable and the product of intense sexual excitement. His behaviour is usually normal until the next paroxysm.'

R. von Krafft-Ebing suggested that lust murder symbolised the act of defloration: 'The perverse urge in murders for pleasure does not solely aim at causing the victim pain and . . . death, but that the real meaning of the action consists in to a certain extent imitating, though perverted into a monstrous and ghastly form, the act of defloration. It is for this reason that an essential component of murders for pleasure is the employment of a sharp cutting weapon. The victim has to be pierced, slit, even chopped up. The correlation between pleasure-murder and defloration is further confirmed by the fact that the chief wounds are inflicted in the stomach region, and in many cases the fatal cuts run from the vagina into the abdomen.'

Jack the Ripper is an obvious example of this sort of murderer. More recent examples include Patrick Byrne, who killed and then mutilated a girl in a YWCA hostel; Michael

Dowdall, who killed and mutilated a prostitute; James Barclay, who, after several violent attacks on women, murdered a prostitute then violently assaulted her; and Neville Heath, who killed and mutilated two women. Byrne, Dowdall, Barclay, and Heath were all diagnosed as being psychopathic.

Neville Heath is one of the clearest examples of the sadistic lust-murderer. Not only did he beat his victims with a whip (common enough in sadomasochistic practices which stop well short of murder) but then mutilated the breasts and abdomen. There is no doubt that Heath derived considerable sexual satisfaction from these revolting acts. We can see in this case both the obsession with breasts observed by several psychoanalysts and perhaps the symbolic defloration noted by Krafft-Ebing.

It seems clear that the Yorkshire Ripper belongs in this category but before we come to any definite conclusion we should look at one or two other types of abnormal murder.

Professor Don Gibbons defines psychopathic killers as 'adults who engage in violent and seemingly meaningless assaults upon others'. He finds that, as children, they often attacked other children, adults, or animals, sometimes with great cruelty. They are defiant, hostile and suspicious of others and frequently see themselves as 'tough' and 'manly'. In almost every case they experienced early and severe rejection by their parents and many lived in institutions or with different foster parents.

Some psychiatrists identify the 'explosive murderer' as a special type. He is a person who normally manages to repress all his emotional feelings but there may come a time, perhaps triggered by some extraordinary situation, when all this repressed emotion wells to the surface in one sudden and uncharacteristic violent outburst. A related approach suggests that he projects his repressed emotions on to another person and then, by killing that person, he is symbolically destroying what he most dislikes in himself. To quote Dr Allen again : 'This explains . . . such cases as those men who kill prostitutes. Firstly he finds his own sexual feelings unacceptable because he has been brought up to the idea that sex is unclean, disgusting and horrible. He projects his sexual feelings into prostitutes and so feels that they are disgusting, dirty, and horrible, because of their sexual behaviour. He cannot, however, suppress his urges indefinitely, and is finally driven to go with one, but kills her in an outburst of fury because of the attributes he has projected on to her.'

It has been suggested that the Ripper has an abnormal hatred of prostitutes, that he is trying to eliminate prostitution. However, most 'explosive murders', whether of prostitutes, or of wives, children, or friends, are 'once only' affairs. The Ripper has killed twelve times, as well as attacking women on other occasions, and not all the victims have been prostitutes. Also, while the explosive murderer may indulge in a violent frenzy of beating or stabbing, the Ripper's actions seem to be more deliberate in character.

One of the most comprehensive studies of abnormal murderers in Britain was carried out by Dr R. Blackburn, Senior Clinical Psychologist at Broadmoor Hospital. He gave personality tests* to fifty-six murderers in Broadmoor. He found they fell into four distinct types.

Type 1 he called 'over-controlled repressors'. These were mild-mannered individuals who normally react to unpleasant and hostile situations by avoidance and denial but, when their inhibitions are finally overcome, they hit out blindly and do not know when to stop hitting. They were older than the other types and tended to kill relatives.

Type 2 he called 'paranoid-aggressives'. These were anxious, hostile and impulsive, and seemed to lack inhibitions against the expression of anti-social values and behaviour. They tended to be somewhat younger than the other murderers and to have a number of criminal convic-

*Using the MMPI (Minnesota Multiphasic Personality Inventory) subjects are shown statements pertaining to aspects of personality which they sort into 'true', 'false' and 'cannot say'. Answers are evaluated in terms of psychiatric categories.

tions. This type did include some sex offenders.

Type 3 he called 'depressed-inhibited'. These men were socially anxious, introverted, depressed, and displayed strong impulse control. They were generally older than average, married, and diagnosed as schizophrenic.

Type 4 he called 'psychopathic'. They were impulsive, extroverted, hostile, and lacking in social anxiety. They were younger and more criminal than the other groups but in every case their victim had been a member of their immediate family (although this was probably a coincidence).

These four types fall into two broad categories: under-controlled offenders (types 2 and 4) with little or no control over their emotional impulses; and over-controlled offenders (types 1 and 3) with, if anything, too much control over whatever aggressive impulses they possess and who are habitually inhibited and unaggressive. When, for some reason, this control snaps there may be an explosion of violence.

It may be useful to mention one further academic study before we apply these theories and findings to the Ripper. Professor Don Gibbons, an American criminologist, argues that the 'Violent Sex Offender' should be considered a special type of criminal, to be distinguished from psycho-pathic offenders, other violent offenders, aggressive rapists, and other sex offenders. Violent sex offenders engage in violent attacks on female victims of an ostensibly sexual character although normal sexual acts may not take place. These attacks are 'usually accompanied by acts of extreme and bizarre violence, such as slashing of the victim, cutting off of breasts, and other activities'. The victim is completely (or relatively) unknown to the offender, either a casual pick-up or a woman surprised or ambushed alone. Offenders do not think of themselves as criminal and generally have no criminal records. They do not come from any particular social class but their family background may be very significant, probably involving repressive sexual notions and possibly some sort of mother–son seduction:

'. . . violent sex offenders probably grow up in family environments which are simultaneously seductive and repressive . . . a basic heterosexual orientation . . . further aroused by a variety of sexually provocative overtures of the mother. Case history documents often note such experiences as the mother sleeping with the son or bathing with him after he has become a physically mature young male. It would be surprising if the offender could repress completely any feeling of sexual arousal that emanated from these experiences. At the same time, the youth is prevented from overt demonstrations of arousal partly because of the incest taboo . . . The mother in many cases probably verbalises about sexual responsiveness in ways which treat it as dirty, evil and something not to be openly acknowledged. This sort of interactive process may well produce individuals who are carriers of combined themes of lust and aggression in pronounced form. Their hostility-charged sexual actions represent the extreme form of the erotic-aggressive syndrome.'**

So, we are presented with a range of options: the Ripper could be a psychopath, a sadist, an explosive murderer, an under-controlled killer, an over-controlled killer or a violent sex offender. These categories are taken from various authorities who all have different approaches: some of them overlap with others, while some are mutually exclusive. However, if we now match what we know about the Ripper's behaviour against these categories, we may be able to build up a tentative psychological picture. Obviously we can only generalise; until he is caught no one can know anything about him for certain. Moreover, since the police, for obvious reasons, are withholding detailed descriptions of the killings and other information, it is not possible to do more than speculate.

**Erotic-aggressive syndrome: the idea that sex and violence are so often associated in modern culture that ideas which link eroticism and cruelty are sometimes learned by young men as part of their sexual knowledge, resulting in a range of behaviour from minor force in sexual encounters through rape to lust-murder.

From what we know of the Ripper, is he a psychopath? As we have seen, psychopaths are impulsive, egocentric, guiltless, loveless and aggressive, while at the same time they may show considerable superficial charm. They are not easily aroused to states of excitement or fear and they seem incapable of anticipating the consequences of their own actions, either to themselves or others. In a nutshell, they appear to lack both a conscience and most of the normal human emotions.

It seems certain that the Ripper speaks to his victims and walks and sometimes drives with them some way before he kills them. We can therefore conclude that he possesses at least a veneer of charm and normality; he is not some Frankenstein monster shambling out of the night. He is clearly aggressive and also egocentric. From the evidence of the tape recording and the letters he seems to enjoy his notoriety and to revel in publicity, boasting of what he has already done and what he intends to do.

The tape recording may indicate other things. The mere fact that it was made and sent points to an impulsive, egocentric, confident, even contemptuous nature. Common sense should warn any murderer of the danger of drawing attention to himself in this fashion. Neither the content of the message nor the tone of the voice betray the slightest hint of any guilt or remorse, any realisation of the enormity of his crimes. On the contrary, the tone is bantering and slightly humorous, taunting the police with their inability to catch him, and promising to carry on.

Finally, the calmness with which the killings appear to be carried out, even in more or less public places, and the fact that he has returned, perhaps more than once, to the scene of a murder to carry out further mutilations or to move the body, point to a man who does not or cannot anticipate danger. Although this may be the result of an overwhelming obsession which blocks out everything else, it is more likely to indicate a typical psychopathic personality. In addition, the emotional stimulation he derives from the killings, followed by the publicity and police activity may be the only excitement he can feel. According to a forensic psychiatrist speaking on London Weekend Television, 'The publicity is getting better for him. I think it's very definitely on the cards he will become more flamboyant.'

All this is strong evidence that the Ripper is a psychopath. However, we do not know if he manifests any of the other symptoms of psychopathy. We cannot tell if he is generally untruthful, unreliable, and insincere; or if he has any insight into his own condition, although it seems probably not. Above all we do not know if he has any real capacity for love and affection. Is he a good friend? A good husband and father? None of these questions can be answered until he is caught.

Is he a sadist? The answer to this must be an unqualified yes. The evidence that he is not just a sadist, but the most extreme type of sadist – a lust murderer – comes from what we know of the manner of the killings. It appears that he kills his victims or renders them unconscious with a hammer blow to the head. Then, either immediately or, in some cases returning hours or days later, he strips the body, scattering the clothes some distance. Next he sets to work mutilating the body with a knife, concentrating, as far as we can tell, on the breasts and abdomen. Finally he hides the body where it will eventually be found. Indeed, there is evidence that on one occasion he returned some days later and moved the body to a more exposed position where it was certain to be found. There seems to be no evidence of sexual intercourse with the victim, either when alive or after death.

If this speculative reconstruction of his behaviour is accurate, then he fits into the category of sadistic lust murderer. With the characteristic mutilation of the breasts and perhaps the symbolic defloration of which Krafft-Ebing writes. Also, the repetition of the killings points to the obsessive-compulsive element noted by Dr Allen. We do not know for certain that he derives any sexual satisfaction from killing and mutilating women. Unless the police have some evidence for this (such as semen stains on or near the victim), this is something we cannot know until he is caught. However, given the parallels with other examples of lust-murder, we can assume that he does derive some pleasure from his activities. Lust-murder is a sub-type of sadism in which the pleasure lies in the act of killing itself and in the subsequent infliction of mutilations. It is possible that the act of killing, or even simple assault, is sometimes sufficient to induce sexual gratification. When this fails the murderer may resort to mutilation of the body after death to achieve the same end.

Krafft-Ebing gives a good example of this: 'Vincente Verzeni . . . said that it had given him an indescribably pleasant (sensual) feeling to commit them [three assaults and two murders]. It was all the same to him in this respect whether the women were old or young, ugly or beautiful. Generally, he said, the mere act of throttling had satisfied him, and then . . . he had let his victims live on – in the two cases he mentioned [two women strangled then characteristically mutilated] he said his sexual satisfaction delayed coming on until the victims were dead . . . His physical strength had been enormous, he said, at these moments of supreme delight. He had never been a fool in carrying out his crimes; he had never had any perception of things around him . . . He always had extremely pleasant feelings afterwards, a sensation of great satisfaction, never any remorse or conscience.'

Is the Ripper an 'explosive murderer'? Probably not. It is highly unlikely that this type of murderer who is generally rather repressed and inhibited would deliberately draw attention to himself with a boastful tape-recorded message sent to the police. Nor would he kill over and over again, nor would he return to the scene of the crime to mutilate the body.

It is true that explosive murderers sometimes kill prostitutes, but although the Ripper concentrates on prostitutes, probably because they are readily available and easy victims, he has also assaulted and killed women who have not been prostitutes.

It is possible that the Ripper is both a sadist *and* an explosive killer. He may manage to suppress his sadistic tendencies most of the time, but occasionally, perhaps after drinking or taking drugs, they prove too strong to suppress and break through into consciousness. When this occurs in a situation where there is a readily available victim (for example a pub frequented by prostitutes – almost all his victims had been drinking in pubs) then he may set out to enjoy himself sadistically but soon loses control and kills.

However, this is highly unlikely. He appears to go out fully equipped, with instruments of murder, for a killing. He boasts about his killings in letters and tape recordings. There is no evidence of sexual intercourse with his victims – or indeed any contact beyond the initial approach and the subsequent sudden assault. In fact the Ripper's murders, far from being sudden explosions of repressed feelings, appear to be premeditated, calm and deliberate.

There is one final possibility. Perhaps his first-ever assault was (and this is something we may never know if it was not reported to the police) an 'explosive' assault, which may or may not have resulted in murder. This could have given him so much sexual satisfaction that, perhaps to his own surprise, he may have gone on to repeat this behaviour deliberately. This leaves a lot of questions unanswered, but it remains a possibility.

The *Daily Mirror* in June 1979 quoted Dr Stephen Shaw, consultant at Stanley Road Hospital near the murder hunt headquarters in Wakefield. It stated that Dr Shaw had told police that he believed the Ripper to be an 'over-controlled aggressive psychopath'. Is he over-controlled or under-controlled? The over-controlled category overlaps with that of the explosive murderer. They are mild-mannered and inhibited, often introverted and sometimes depressed, and normally have strong control over their emotions. My research suggests that the Ripper does not really fit this description.

The under-controlled category includes psychopaths, whom we have already discussed, and 'paranoid-aggressives'. Of the paranoid-aggressives, Blackburn says, 'Symptomatically, this is the most disturbed of the four groups, the overall profile being distinctly abnormal . . . Anxiety and hostility are at a very high level, significantly higher, in fact, than in any other group. The members of this group also appear to be impulsive and prone to act out, but at the same time are socially anxious and somewhat introverted. They are generally younger than all others. They tend to be unmarried, have a previous criminal record and are the least intelligent . . . A few are classified as psychopathic, but the majority as mentally ill, over half being diagnosed as schizophrenic. Their victims are mostly strangers or casual acquaintances and of the seven homicides with an overt sexual component four fell in this group.'

This description has one or two things in common with the Ripper but in general, and particularly in the emphasis of introversion and social anxiety, this seems to be a different type. However, the Ripper could possibly be a sadistic paranoid-aggressive?

Finally, is the Ripper a 'violent sex offender'? The answer to this is clearly yes. Of all the possible categories this most clearly matches what we know of him. It tells us very little about him, but if we accept Gibbons' description it may tell us something of his probable family background. The Ripper is obviously one of that small minority of criminals who is mentally abnormal, although he may appear, superficially, to be as normal as you or I. The popular image of the Ripper as a salivating werewolf out of a Hammer film only serves to impede detection. We must recognise that the killer is a real man living a real life situation. We can also conclude that he is almost certainly a sadist and probably a psychopath. In addition he fits the criminological category 'violent sex offender'. It is also possible, although unlikely, that he is an over-controlled, 'explosive' murderer with sadistic tendencies. In fact he appears to be a sadistic, psychopathic, violent sex offender, probably from a very disturbed, rejecting, and sexually repressive family background. He probably derives some sexual pleasure from his activities as well as a feeling of excitement. In common with other psychopaths and violent sex offenders, the chances are that he is quite young – perhaps in his early thirties.

With one or two exceptions, notably Peter Kurten who has been dealt with in Chapter One, few studies of the 'lustmord' or sadistic phenomenon are available to the public or, for that matter, to scholars. I attach to this section, therefore, some brief notes on a selection of the more noteworthy cases which appear to have certain similarities to the Ripper case. I am indebted to Professor Terrence Morris for suggesting appropriate examples to me, some of these being drawn from his book, *A Calendar of Murder* (Terrence Morris and Louis Blum Cooper, 1964).

The inclusion of Marcel Petiot is justified on the grounds that he exhibits many of the traits of psychopathic personality we have investigated. Indeed if we take Professor Cleckley's definition of a psychopath it is rather like a mirror held up to Petiot himself : 'Superficial charm and good intelligence, absence of signs of irrational thinking, absence of nervousness, unreliability, untruthfulness and insincerity, lack of remorse or shame.'

The examples of Kurten and Petiot prove, if it was necessary to do so, that mass homicide and sadism take no account of national boundaries. Indeed, despite the Ripper, these phenomenon seem to occur more frequently in continental Europe and the United States.

The Yorkshire Ripper is linked in the public mind with the two 'Moors Murderers', Myra Hindley and Ian Brady; the 'Black Panther' Donald Neilson; and 'Mad Billy', William Hughes, who tortured and killed a Derbyshire family of four in 1977 before the police gunned him down. The examples given below are, however, more proximate in terms of what we take to be the nature of the killer's psychology.

In 1961 Edward David Sims, a carpenter's mate, walked into the offices of the *Daily Mirror* with a plastic bag containing human parts and confessed to the double murder of a young couple on marshland near Gravesend. He strangled the boy and threw him in a dyke, then he strangled and subsequently mutilated the girl before she too was thrown in the dyke.

At Maidstone Assizes doctors described Sims as a long-standing aggressive psychopath with grossly perverted sexual inclinations. His crime 'was almost an end product of the insidious degeneration of his perverted instincts. His abnormality developed from morbid fantasy into pathological obsession.'

In 1960 an Irish labourer, Patrick Joseph Byrne, aged twenty-seven, confessed to the murder of Stephanie Baird, twenty-nine, in a Birmingham YWCA hostel. Byrne prowled round the hostel as a 'peeping Tom', and when Stephanie spotted him at her window he burst in and strangled her. He cut off a breast and the head of the girl with a table knife and inflicted other mutilations. Byrne was not caught until he confessed to the police six or seven weeks later. Undisputed medical evidence was given at the trial that Byrne was an aggressive psychopath with a long history of sexual abnormality.

Michael Douglas Dowdall, a nineteen-year-old Welsh guardsman, went with a thirty-one-year-old prostitute to her home in Kilburn; a quarrel arose and Dowdall battered the woman to death. After her death he forced two coat-hangers into her body and mutilated her. He was eventually arrested after a similar attack on another woman eleven months later. She survived, and the police were able to circulate a description. Fingerprints found at the woman's home tallied with those found at the scene of the Kilburn murder, and also with prints discovered at a series of houses in the London area which had been broken into and from which property had been stolen.

133

At the trial the Principal Medical Officer of Brixton described Dowdall as a psychopathic personality, liable to aggressive and violent behaviour without sufficient cause. He was also described as a 'difficult and precocious' type, and his commanding officer said he seemed to have delusions of grandeur. Dowdall had attempted to hang himself two years previously.

The theme of psychopathic disorder comes out strongly in all three cases. What is also interesting is that Dowdall eluded arrest for eleven months and was only then apprehended after another vicious attack on a woman who survived and was able to give the police a description. The other two men both came forward with confessions, which is often the only way in which the police can clear up these matters. At the time of writing there seems to be some evidence that the Yorkshire Ripper may come forward with a confession or at least offer enough clues to enable the police eventually to discover his identity.

A friend of mine remembers Neville Heath in immediate post-war London. Good-looking, somewhat crude, surrounded by a group of sycophantic admirers, Heath wore the uniform of the South African Air Force with DFC and Africa Star. He was glamorous, a high roller and attractive to women.

In the summer of 1946 Heath committed two terrible motiveless murders within a few days. His previous career typifies that of vicious sadist and psychopath. At school in Wimbledon he behaved as a bully and was known to torture animals. His criminal career began early and was mainly related to theft, offences such as breaking and entering, larceny, fraud, cheque bouncing and taking money from friends and hotels. Before the war he was sentenced to a period of Borstal training and was later released in order that he could join the Army. It was typical of his outrageous bravado that he revisited the Borstal where he gave a pep talk to the boys on the lines of 'how I made good – so can you'.

During his wartime career Heath managed to get himself

court-martialled and dismissed from three services, the Army, the Royal Air Force and the South African Air Force. Heath was a poseur who tried to pass himself off as an important personage, on one occasion assuming the title of Earl of Dudley. When in South Africa he managed to insinuate himself into affluent circles, he married a wealthy wife and had one child by her. He shortly deserted her and subsequently blackmailed her family over the matter of her divorce. Nevertheless even after his trial and conviction for a terrible murder Heath's wife was reported as saying 'there is so much goodness in him'.

Heath's two victims were: Mrs Margery Aimee Brownell Gardner, aged thirty-two, described as a film extra, who met her death at the Pembridge Court Hotel, Notting Hill on 30th June 1946; and Miss Doreen Marshall, aged twenty-one, who was killed at Branksome Dene Chine, Bournemouth, on 4th July.

Margery Gardner had previously been rescued from Heath after a savage assault in a West End hotel where she was bruised and beaten, only a month before her murder. Remarkably, she was prepared to join him again for a night in a hotel. She must have known she would be beaten again and was certainly aware that Heath carried a riding switch for the purpose.

Mrs Gardner died of suffocation, maybe by having her head pushed into a pillow, but before this she had sustained appalling injuries. She had been beaten with a woven thong (the riding switch with a metal tip and a silver knob). Seventeen lashes were to be seen on her front and back. She had been bitten on the upper part of her body, and in the lower part there was a long deep wound. Her face showed marks of violence. Her ankles were tied and there were tie marks on her wrists, which had later been released.

Miss Doreen Marshall's body was found under a rhododendron bush at Branksome Dene Chine, Bournemouth. Her throat had been cut, which was the cause of death. Bruises to the head and left temple had been made after death. There was a long deep vertical cut in the front of the body, deep cuts across the chest and other terrible mutilations.

Heath's trial was held at a time when the outcome of the Nuremberg Trials was being awaited. Dr W. H. D. Hubert was called by the defence. He said Heath was 'of a type born with a deficient moral sense, who would commit any crime or a wide range of crimes'. He believed that at the time of the murders Heath felt that what he was doing was actually right. Dr Hubert said Heath had : 'no appreciation of what other people would think of his behaviour after committing these crimes, he behaved in quite a casual manner, considering his intelligence . . . There was evidence of a general moral degeneracy.'

The trial judge was hostile to Dr Hubert's analysis, which was in conflict with the testimony of the prison medical officers. The defence of moral insanity failed and Heath was sentenced to death by hanging.

According to prison officers in Pentonville, Heath was largely indifferent to his fate, and did not in the event bother to appeal. He refused to receive a visit from his mother on the grounds that he wished her to remember him from better times.

An interesting sidelight on Heath's character was his love of uniform. While in prison he told his warders : 'I wore an RAF tie during the first days of my trial, but I did not wear it on the day the verdict was expected. Whatever they think of me in the outside world, I am proud of my association with the Royal Air Force, and I made up my mind that I would not wear the RAF tie at the last knockings.'

France, it has been said, is the traditional home of Blue-beards, and among these Dr Marcel Petiot can undoubtedly be said to be pre-eminent. He is untypical of other cases mentioned in this section in that greed and financial gain figures as one of the motives for his slayings. On the other hand his career and personality point up many of the characteristics we find in the other examples.

The sadistic psychopath is best calculated to flourish in a war situation. A high proportion of this small group of grossly disordered psychotic killers seems to be attracted to the concept of uniform, and as we have seen with Neville Heath, war-time offers great opportunity for fraud, deception and rapid promotion.

Dr Marcel Petiot was quick to recognise the opportunities presented by the German occupation of France during World War II, during the course of which it is thought that he may have killed as many as a hundred victims. Petiot, who sought sadistic gratification from his murders, also derived very considerable financial reward from the exploitation of his victims.

Petiot was born in 1897 in Auxerre, a French country village one hundred miles south of Paris; he displayed brilliance at school and a high delinquent tendency to petty larceny. He conducted cruel experiments on animals and was thought to show an unhealthy interest in methods of torturing the human body. In his teens he was committing burglary and other offences around the village. Conscripted in 1917, Petiot was later discharged from the army with instructions to undergo psychoneurosis treatment, and spent some of the next two years in a lunatic asylum.

In 1921 Petiot qualified as a doctor and took up a practice in the small town of Villeneuve-sur-Yonne, where he stood as a local government candidate. Petiot demonstrated considerable charm, particularly towards women, and was also remembered for numerous small acts of kindness. Such was his popularity that by 1928 he had been elected Mayor. Although popular, Marcel Petiot was the subject of persistent gossip, and had a lurid reputation. It was rumoured that he indulged in sadistic practices and that women were heard crying out in agony from the Petiot menage. It was observed nevertheless that the women would return willingly to the same premises. Along with this Petiot seems to have continued in his career of petty larceny, and also as a peeping Tom. At about this time he married Georgette, an attractive daughter of a Paris restaurateur who was to remain loyal right up to the end.

In 1930 Petiot was arrested for stealing, in his capacity

as Mayor, from the municipal store. After serving a short term of imprisonment, he moved to Paris where he established a practice. At this time Petiot had a reputation as an abortionist and was also known to prescribe drugs to addicts.

It is thought that Petiot may have disposed of at least two women before the war. His motive on these occasions seems to have been that the women were causing him personal embarrassment either as a result of accusations of paternity or of medical malpractice. However, it was only after the German occupation of Paris that Petiot established himself as a mass murderer of monster proportions. His opportunity arose from the desire of Jews and others to escape from the Occupation. Petiot represented himself as a liaison officer with the Resistance, who could arrange an escape route to safety abroad. Individuals and families seeking his assistance would go to premises which Petiot described as a private hospital. This they believed was the first stage of their journey to freedom. Here they would be vaccinated by the doctor, who in fact injected them with poison. Dr Petiot would then observe the agonising deaths of his victims through a viewing panel in a sealed chamber from which they struggled unavailingly to escape. Attached to this 'private hospital' was a furnace in which Petiot used to destroy his victims after he had chopped them up.

Dr Petiot's activities eventually came to the notice of the Gestapo, who in fact imprisoned him for a while. Presumably he was able to persuade them that he was only doing on a small scale the work of extermination which the Gestapo was itself engaged upon in Poland and Germany. After seven months he was released and once again the chimney of his furnace began to issue forth greasy black smoke, the smell of which reminded old soldiers of the trenches during the First World War.

In March 1944 the chimneys of Petiot's furnace caught fire whilst the doctor was attending to his patients in another part of Paris. By the time of Petiot's arrival on the scene, police and firemen were attempting to estimate how many people had been killed from the piles of remains they had found in the cellar. Petiot was ready with his explanation: he confided to the police that he was operating a disposal unit on behalf of the Resistance. It was his job, he explained, to dispose of traitors who had been condemned to death for collaborating with the enemies of France. Later, he was to declare, 'If I deserve anything at all it is a medal, not a prison cell.'

The Sureté eventually caught up with Petiot after the Liberation. By this time he was back in uniform posing as a Capitaine Henri Valery working in an interrogation centre where he had already become noted for his sadistic approach in questioning prisoners. When approached he said, 'Do hurry with your questions, there is a war on, you know. I'm needed at the battlefield.'

In March 1946 Petiot was found guilty of twenty-four of the twenty-seven murders with which he was charged.

CHAPTER ELEVEN

What is the Ripper like?

From the beginning of the inquiry police began to build up a psychological picture of the killer. These characteristics have been dealt with in foregoing chapters. However, as more forensic information came into their possession the police were able to establish certain personal characteristics of the murderer which were often at variance with public speculation as to his identity, his origins and his employment. It was noticeable that members of the public who offered an opinion would point to a social category within which they did not include themselves. The prostitute who thought the killer must be either a top policeman or an eminent surgeon was by no means alone in that view, a popular theory also at the time of the Whitechapel murders in the 1880s.

A brewery checker who claimed intimate knowledge of the victims' wounds and who stated that the killer had scattered stones on their eviscerated bodies, said confidently that the killer must be drawn from 'class' people. Judging the killer to be a motorist, a point on which everyone seemed agreed, he was able to indicate the killer's routes home to the better-off suburbs of Leeds, inhabitated as they are by 'class' people. These suburbs lie mainly to the North of the city, places like Bramhope, Weetwood, Moor Allerton, Shadwell and Thorner.

During the long course of the inquiry, the killer, or in some cases witnesses later eliminated after police questioning, have been described in a variety of conflicting and confusing ways. At various times the police have been said to be looking for 'tall', 'average' or 'fairly short' men; 'dark-haired', 'blond', 'ginger-haired'; with 'enlarged or puffy hand', etc. During the investigations into Helen Rytka's death a 'business-man type' was being sought, presumably the occupant of one of the expensive cars that cruise up and down Great Northern Street, Huddersfield, looking for prostitutes.

The age range of the killer has been given as anything from twenties to fifty-five, and as late as July 1979 there was no precise information on this point. The only consistent description of the killer has been that he is a male white.

Maureen Long's description of her attacker was that he was 'six foot tall and well made, with wiry blond hair, thick eyebrows, puffed cheeks and noticeably large hands.'

Marilyn Moore, another survivor, described her attacker as 'good-looking with come-to-bed eyes'. The man had a square jaw and a Zapata-like moustache.

On 2nd December 1978 the *Daily Mail* published an artist's impression based on Marilyn Moore's description of the Ripper. The police also issued an Identikit picture, based on the same description, of a youngish looking man with long hair. This was subsequently withdrawn as misleading. At the time of Josephine Whitaker's murder a man of similar description was seen in a parked car in Saville Park. He was wearing a tartan check shirt open at the front, tartan jacket with a light-coloured fur collar and was of scruffy appearance.

On 30th June 1979, the *Daily Express* published a 'portrait' of the Ripper on its front page, a somewhat stunted, bearded individual wearing a donkey jacket. The figure bore these labels in boxes:

speedy, confident and obsessive

Sunderland accent
five foot ten inches tall
white
age 30–45
strongly built
blood group AB
single and living alone?

working in Yorkshire?
uses work bench equipment to mutilate his victims,
wears heavy industrial boots.

The following day the *Sunday People* published their own portrait of the killer, clean-shaven and of less rough appearance.

By 1979 forensic findings at the scene of the murder of Josephine Whitaker, together with information derived from letters believed to have been sent to the police by the Ripper, suggested that he was engaged in some form of engineering work, and that he could well be a manual worker.

In April 1979 Mr Oldfield said he had 'a considerable impression of the person we are seeking . . . I believe him to be white, between thirty and fifty-five years old, at least average to above average height, an artisan or manual worker, either skilled or semi-skilled, with engineering or mechanical connections and possibly a skilled machine tool fitter, electrical or mechanical engineer'.

By this time the police knew a great deal about the Ripper. Assuming the tape to be genuine they would be able to produce a voice recording at the trial. Again, assuming the genuineness of the letters, they had specimens of the killer's handwriting and information derived from the graphologists' interpretation of the specimens. Linguistic experts who examined the tapes were confident that the murderer derived his accent from Sunderland (south of the Tyne) or Newcastle-upon-Tyne. Judging from his voice the killer appeared to be a man of some education, possibly in technical skills up to perhaps ONC or HNC level. The letters revealed poor grammatical skill and spelling mistakes, though these could, of course, be deliberate. Saliva tests of the glue on envelopes also revealed the killer's blood group to be AB, very rare for a white male.

The letters from the Ripper had been posted in the North-East, two in March 1978 and one in March 1979. These, together with the killer's North-East accent, seemed to establish a strong link with that region and suggested that the Ripper could have been working in the area at the time the letters were posted. The following appeal was published in the June 1979 issue of *Engineering* :

Mr Oldfield has now made this appeal : 'I would like the management of firms in Yorkshire engaged in machine tool manufacture, engineering, including electrical or marine engineering, plant and machinery maintenance, or similar trades, to examine their records and let me know whether they have business connections with the North-East. Also whether any of their employees – skilled, semi-skilled or unskilled – were engaged on work in the North-East or Tyneside area on any of the following dates : 7th or 8th March 1978, 12th or 13th March 1978 and the 22nd or 23rd March 1979.

I would like firms in the North-East, including Tyneside, to let me know whether employees from firms in Yorkshire were engaged on maintenance, repair or installation work on their premises on any of those dates.

It would be helpful to know from employers in Yorkshire who are engaged in the engineering field, in its broadest terms, details of employees who were off work on the above dates.

By June 1979 the image of the killer in police minds

suggested that he was somewhat scruffy in appearance, wearing work boots or Wellingtons. It was also thought that he was driving a fairly old model car, quite possibly one maintained by himself.

Mr Oldfield also thought that the killer was being protected consciously or unconsciously by someone, perhaps a wife or elderly mother. It was thought that they could be very dependent for support on the killer and therefore very reluctant to voice any suspicion of him. It is possible, for example, that a wife, like that of the Black Panther, could be living in fear of the killer and terrified of going to the police. Sir Melville Macnaughten, in charge of Scotland Yard in 1894 and whose duty it was to close the file on Jack the Ripper, concluded: 'From private information I have little doubt but that his own family (referring to the prime suspect, Druitt) suspected this man as being the Whitechapel murderer.' It is thought that Druitt may have confessed to his brother who did what he could to conceal the information. This illustrates the fact that relations may be too ashamed to come forward. Again, in the case of Peter Kurten, when he realised that the police had caught up with him and told his wife of the dreadful catalogue of crimes which he had committed, mainly while she was working overtime, her reaction was: 'What is to become of me?' It was at Kurten's own insistence that she went to the police in order to claim the reward money, so that she would be able to support herself as a widow. Kurten was in fact surprised at the speed with which she acted. He had no intention of giving himself up straight away and was in fact planning to fit in a further murder at the time of his arrest.

It is by no means impossible that the killer has not given rise to any suspicion on the part of a relative. This was the case with Kurten; indeed, so meticulous was he in cleaning up after his crimes that forensic investigators were only able to discover traces of the victims' blood in his trouser linings. In this connection it was thought that the Yorkshire killer may have had undetectable means of industrial waste disposal at hand, which would enable him to get rid of soiled garments or weapons.

The rest was mere speculation. One theory that was aired was that he could be a storekeeper, which would give him the opportunity to secrete implements and tools, weapons used in his murders. Another popular theory was that he might well have worked in the public service as a special constable, for example, like Christie, mass murderer of 10 Rillington Place, or as an auxiliary fireman. The basis for the latter suggestion was that there is a strong association between firelighting and other psychopathic behaviour. It has incidentally been observed that a worrying percentage of firemen are attracted to arson.

CHAPTER TWELVE

Jack the Stripper

Typical of the many routine inside page headlines that appeared in the national newspapers on Monday 3rd February 1964 was this by no means exclusive one, featured on page twelve of the London *Evening Standard*: 'Thames Nude – It Looks Like Murder, says CID.'

Little did the readers of this piece realise at the time that the finding of this Thames Nude was to prelude a series of savage killings in West London that over the next twelve months were to receive more sustained publicity than any other mass murder since Jack the Ripper's most publicised of all murders three-quarters of a century before. They were also to lead the Metropolitan Police to mount one of the biggest manhunts in its history, and provide Scotland Yard with one of its most sensational cases. The case in question was the London Nude Murders, the murderer was also salaciously, though descriptively, dubbed by the popular press, 'Jack the Stripper'.

The series of killings bears many obvious similarities to those of the Yorkshire Ripper and provides a useful precedent for surmise on the Yorkshire murders. In particular they throw light on the immense problems confronting a modern police force attempting to capture such a killer in contemporary society. They also provide useful clues, obviously conjectural, as to possible behavioural patterns of the killer himself. These 'Stripper' clues become doubly significant if taken in tandem with the Whitechapel murders.

The Whitechapel murders have been described already. We shall look later to these parallels and their possible relevance, having examined in some detail the series of murders that occurred in London between February 1964 and February 1965.

The body that was discovered on the Thames foreshore near Hammersmith Bridge on Sunday 2nd February 1964 and reported in the press the next day was that of Hannah Tailford, a thirty-year-old prostitute from Thurlby Road, West Norwood. The corpse was completely naked except for her stockings, which were round her ankles, and her frilly panties which were stuffed into her mouth; there was no sign of the rest of her clothing, which was never found. Pathological examination by Dr Donald Teare revealed some bruising round the jaw which could have resulted from a fall or accident and she was also found to be pregnant. At the subsequent inquest at Hammersmith, in the absence of other information, the Coroner, Mr Gavin Thurston, had no alternative but to return an open verdict.

Since something like a hundred bodies are found in or around the Thames each year, most of them suicides or accidents, there was nothing particularly remarkable about this case. This was borne out by the investigation carried out by Detective Inspector Frank Ridge of the Thames Police CID and Detective Chief Inspector Ben Devonald, who, despite questioning hundreds of people, could come up with nothing of importance other than fairly routine facts relating to her life-style.

The facts were that she had arrived in London from Heddon-on-the-Wall in Northumberland and had since used a number of aliases, among them Anne Taylor, Teresa Bell and Anne and Hannah Lynch; the last name was derived from the man she had lived with for some time, Walter Lynch, by whom she had a three-year-old daughter. More interestingly there was evidence that she went to porno-graphic parties attended by diplomats in Kensington and Mayfair. It was also discovered that she kept photographic equipment in a flat she rented for use with her clients, which indicated that either pornographic picture-taking was among these clients' perversions or else she may have been involved in a blackmail racket : this was initially thought to be significant, but was later discounted.

Despite the lack of hard evidence and the open coroner's verdict, the police felt that Hannah Tailford had been murdered. This theory was reinforced when, just over two-and-a-half months later, another naked body was found in very similar circumstances little more than 300 yards from the spot where Hannah Tailford had been discovered. This body, discovered on 8th April on the mud flats at Dukes Meadows, Chiswick, was that of a tiny, five foot tall, twenty-five-year-old blonde from Denbigh Road, Ealing, called Irene Lockwood. Like Hannah Tailford she was found to be pregnant and all her clothes were missing. Her body had been in the river for approximately twenty-four hours before its discovery and a tattoo reading 'John in Memory' on her right arm helped to identify her. It was also ascertained that she had been strangled.

Detective Superintendent Frank Davis, working from his headquarters at Shepherd's Bush police station, like his colleague Frank Ridge, came up with no hard evidence of any kind. It was established that Irene had come from Lincolnshire, used the alias Sandra Russell, took pep pills, had been involved in pornographic film rackets, and had been beaten up several times for attempting to blackmail clients with compromising photographs. By a most strange coincidence her partner in these enterprises, another prostitute called Vicki Pender, had also been strangled to death almost exactly a year before by her ex-paratroop boyfriend, Colin Welt Fisher. Interestingly, when first interviewed by the police, Fisher had produced a false alibi involving Irene Lockwood.

With so little to go on the police suspected that she might have been murdered by one of her blackmail victims, or else perhaps the ponces behind her rackets had silenced her for 'freelancing'. Although not without foundation these suspicions were mainly speculative.

Investigations were continuing along these lines when, to the amazement of all concerned, a fifty-four-year-old bachelor called Kenneth Archibald walked in to Notting Hill police station and confessed to the murder of Irene Lockwood. Archibald was charged with the crime and sent for trial so that a jury could decide on his case. He repeated his confession twice, once verbally and once in writing in great detail. This confession is of particular interest since the police took it far more seriously than the usual false confessions that often accompany murder investigations. Obviously, for a time at least, they considered the confession to be genuine. All this very well illustrates the problems the police have in deciding whether information they are given is genuine or not (this applies as much to a tape or letter as to a confession, and it also illustrates how misleading reliance on circumstantial evidence can be). Bearing all this in mind, it is worth looking at Kenneth Archibald's confession in some detail. This is what happened.

The 27th April 1964, the day he made his confession, had been an exceptionally hectic and most unwelcome one for the stockily-built ex-Army and Merchant Navy caretaker of the fashionable Holland Park Lawn Tennis Club in Addison Road, for early in the morning the club was broken into and £30 stolen, which he duly reported. Later in the day he appeared at Marlborough Street Magistrates Court to answer allegations concerning the theft of a hearing-aid and the case was adjourned. Afterwards he went drinking with some friends, and when they commented on his depressed state of mind, referring to his hearing-aid problem, he replied: 'It's more serious than that, you don't know how serious it is.' He then made his way to Notting Hill police station and told the duty officer, 'I have come to give myself up.' To the reply that he was referring to the Tennis Club break-in he answered, 'No, I pushed the girl into the river . . . you know, the blonde Lockwood at Chiswick.' Later a police superintendent said of the meeting, 'I took a statement under caution which was in fact an admission.' He continued to 'help the police with their inquiries' for a further three days and on 1st May was remanded in custody until 8th May.

The gist of his confession, which he rigidly adhered to, was that he had picked Irene Lockwood up in a Chiswick pub and taken her down to the river, where she demanded payment in advance; whereupon he lost his temper with her, put his hands round her throat and throttled her. Having taken off her clothes he pushed her into the river and later burnt the clothes. His description of these clothes was apparently extremely accurate as was it of her accent, which implied at least that he could have met her.

This suspicion was strongly reinforced by the fact that he had already been linked earlier with Irene Lockwood and interviewed in this respect on 9th April, since, on examining the effects supplied by her landlady, the police had found this written in her diary along with the name, address and telephone number of the tennis club: 'Kenny is coming on 2nd April or 3rd, Thursday. He is young and handsome.' At his interview he was shown a photograph of Irene Lockwood but denied knowing her.

Despite the lack of concrete evidence, all this clearly indicated a very strong case against Archibald. Subsequently the diary entry proved to be something of a red herring, although it could be argued, and no doubt was at the time, that it was this that, either consciously or sub-consciously, gave him the idea to make the confession in the first place. The accuracy of his description concerning the clothes and accent is harder to explain, but does indicate how easy it is for somebody who has read the press reports to put two and two together and make well-informed guesses which give the impression to the police that they have information which they do not possess.

All this notwithstanding, Archibald appeared at Acton Magistrates' Court on 15th May charged with the murder of Irene Charlotte Lockwood and was duly sent for trial at the Old Bailey.

With Mr E. J. P. Cussen prosecuting for the Crown and before Mr Justice Nield, Archibald pleaded not guilty. After a six-day trial the jury took forty minutes to acquit him and he was discharged the same day (23rd June). During the trial Archibald said he had never been to the riverside pub that Irene Lockwood used before her death and that he had made his confession in a fit of depression because he was worried about his problems, especially the break-in at the tennis club, and thought he might lose his home and job there. He further said that in making his confession all he meant to do was to seek a 'haven of custody' for himself while he sorted out his troubles. Psychologist Dr Peter Duncan of Maudsley Hospital provided medical evidence and confirmed that he could well have faked the story in a mood of despair.

After his trial Kenneth Archibald told reporters : 'I never really indulged in the gay kind of life that in my confessions I pretended I had led . . . my only real mistake at the tennis club was when I was persuaded by a man to start a late drinking club without the tennis players knowing . . . but when they found out after a party lasting to 4 am they over-looked it and allowed me to keep my job. Naturally that was the end of the drinking club.' Kenneth Archibald's pretended 'gay life' cost him a six-day murder trial and fifty-seven days in custody.

On 24th April, three days before Kenneth Archibald made his confession, this banner headline appeared on the front page of the London *Evening Standard*: 'Nude Mystery – Four Murders Link' (two other murders, those of Gwynneth Rees and Elizabeth Figg murdered in November 1963 and June 1959 respectively were originally linked with the 1964 murders but were subsequently discounted). The report was referring to the discovery of the naked body found in a Brentford alleyway of Helen Barthelemy. Since it was linked from the onset (anyway by the press) with the Tailford and Lockwood murders it is probable, although the body was found three days before his confession, that the subsequent inquiries into the Barthelemy murder lessened the case against Archibald.

Certainly the amount of publicity this latest killing generated, together with the publicity attending the confession and trial of Kenneth Archibald, created a minor hiatus within the Stripper's activities, for it was not until 14th July, nearly three months later, that the next body was discovered.

It was found in a sitting position outside the entrance to a private garage in Berrymead Road, a Chiswick cul-de-sac. The victim was a thirty-year-old Scot called Mary Fleming, lately from Barrow-in-Furness and at the time of her death living on National Assistance in one room with her two children in Lancaster Gardens, W.11. She, too, was discovered completely naked with no sign of her clothing anywhere, and like Helen Barthelemy her teeth were missing, though in this case they were dentures.

There were obvious similarities between these two latest murders, since not only had they both had their teeth interfered with (though, curiously, in Barthelemy's case not as a result of a blow), but also their bodies were both found some way from the river in neighbouring districts, and so placed that they would certainly be discovered very quickly without the slightest attempt to conceal them. In common with the previous cases both had been strangled.

It would appear, however, that Helen Barthelemy had led a somewhat more eventful life than Mary Fleming. Also a Scot, she had left home at sixteen after a convent education to become a circus trapeze artiste. This was followed by a spell on Blackpool's Golden Mile as a stripper and café waitress. It was also known that in August 1962 she had been convicted in Liverpool for enticing a youth on to the Blackpool beach, and with an accomplice robbing him of £20. Her four-year sentence was quashed on appeal and soon after she appeared in London soliciting in the Notting Hill and Shepherd's Bush areas. At the time of her death she was twenty-two, the youngest so far of four victims. Interestingly, she had been warned by the police only a few days before her murder about the dangers of soliciting in Notting Hill. This was because the police were becoming increasingly convinced that the murders had all resulted from casual pick-ups which made the victims such easy prey for the droves of kerb-crawlers that frequented the streets at this time. This theory was strongly reinforced by the latest murders.

So far as the public at large were concerned, it was the death of Helen Barthelemy with its ensuing publicity that made them realise for the first time that a highly dangerous multiple killer was on the prowl in West London.

So far as the police were concerned Helen Barthelemy provided them with their first real clue, which was later reinforced when Mary Fleming's body was examined, for it was found that both bodies had on them tiny particles of dust, which, under microscopic examination, proved also to contain minute paint particles consistent with the type of paint used in the manufacture of certain cars. The inference was obvious, if the police could find the matching paint spray repair shop they might also find the killer. But their problem was enormous, literally like finding the proverbial 'needle' in an area approaching twenty-four square miles, stretching from Paddington to Brentford. To make matters worse it was most difficult for the Metropolitan Police to release more men to the case for already the allocation far exceeded that of a normal murder hunt, and to have increased it further would seriously have hampered the day-to-day work of the force.

However, the police did have one other small clue, for apparently, shortly before Mary Fleming's body was discovered, some house painters on night-shift near Chiswick High Road had heard a car reversing, followed by its door being slammed. They also noticed a man standing by the vehicle who hurriedly jumped in and drove off when he realised he had been seen. Unfortunately, since the men were looking through frosted windows, they were not able to describe the man. However, they did think the car was either an estate or a small van. A motorist was also nearly hit about the same time by a small dark-coloured van as it came out of the cul-de-sac, a fact that he reported to the police. In the event, efforts to trace this small van failed, though the sighting did reinforce the theory that the victims were killed in or near a paint spray shop, kept there for a few days and then taken away in a car or van and dumped.

On 25th November, twenty-three days after the adjourned inquests on Helen Barthelemy and Mary Fleming, at which the Coroner, Mr Harold Broadbridge, had commented that the cases 'were strangely similar', the fifth body, that of twenty-year-old Margaret McGowan, was discovered in a shallow grave in a Hornton Street car park not far from what is now the Kensington and Chelsea Town Hall off Kensington High Street. The pattern was depressingly similar: under five feet two inches tall, naked, clothes destroyed, a tooth missing and death by strangulation. Her body was easily identified by the floral design tattoo bearing the words 'Helen, Mum and Dad' on her left arm.

Quite a bit was known about Margaret McGowan since she had given evidence at the notorious Stephen Ward trial the year before in connection with the Profumo scandal. The alias she used at this time was Frances Brown, although she had a number of others. Originally from Glasgow, she lived in Shepherd's Bush and was the mother of three illegitimate children.

It was also known that on the day that she disappeared (23rd October) she had been soliciting with another girl called Kim Taylor, who later testified that they had picked up two men in separate cars in the Portobello Road, and that it was agreed among them that they should all meet up at Chiswick Green. The cars became separated in the traffic and Margaret was never seen alive again. On the strength of Kim Taylor's evidence, Identikit pictures of the two men were issued to the press with an appeal for the men to come forward – neither did so. Likewise, a thorough investigation of all those connected with the Stephen Ward case revealed nothing.

Exactly a fortnight after the anniversary of the discovery of the Stripper's first victim, his sixth and last, Bridget (Bridie) O'Hara was discovered in thick undergrowth behind a small work shed on the Heron Trading Estate in Acton. The man who found her, Mr Ernest Beauchamp, thought, as did the discoverer of Mary Fleming's body, that she was a tailor's dummy. Inevitably the victim was again less than five feet two inches tall, her clothing had disappeared, she was naked, some of her teeth were missing and she had been strangled. Once again a tattoo, heart-shaped with 'Mick' inscribed within, helped to identify her. A most interesting aspect was that the body was partially mummified and was in an extremely good state of preservation. Similar paint-impregnated dust particles were also found on the body.

Reaction to this murder by the media was immediate; grave concern was expressed as to why the police had failed to capture the killer after so long. It was also feared that he would shortly strike again, since by now it was possible to discern some sort of pattern with the killings. For it seemed that they occurred in cycles of approximately ten weeks, with an odd pair-by-pair similarity. The first two had been dumped in the Thames, the second two dumped openly where they were certain to be discovered, and the final two hidden in relatively out-of-the-way spots.

The police shared these views and were equally quick to react, for immediately the highly experienced Detective Chief Superintendent John Du Rose was brought back from holiday to head the investigation. He had at his disposal the two hundred-strong CID murder force, supplemented by a hundred people from the uniformed branch. He had in addition the services of the newly-formed three hundred-strong Special Patrol Group. As John Du Rose recalls in his book *Murder was my Business*: 'I wanted the whole of West London to be flooded with policemen – and it was.'

Two lines of attack were open to Du Rose: one to attempt to catch the killer at source at the point of pick-up, the other to find the paint-spray repair shop and trace him from there. He pursued them both.

In pursuing the first option all the most likely 'pick-up' points in the Bayswater, Notting Hill and Shepherd's Bush areas were constantly patrolled throughout the night. A system of 'flagging' was introduced whereby the same car in an area more than once became suspect, and if it appeared three times the driver was questioned. Policewomen were disguised as tarts and 'solicited' in the most obvious places. This demanded great courage on the part of the girls concerned, and many of them were amazed by the number of 'clients' they attracted; they were even more amazed by the extraordinarily kinky things they were asked to do with these people.

One interesting aspect is the shock and surprise which was expressed by the police at the bourgeois appearance of the people they were required to interview. Contrary to expectation they were well-off, well educated and socially well connected. The police seemed to be making the presumption that vice was confined to the lower classes – which seems particularly strange at a time immediately following the Profumo scandal. It is perhaps worth remembering in this context that the main suspect following the Whitechapel murders was an old Wykehamist and an Oxonian.

Despite this massive operation nothing of significance was turned up. However, the operation concerning the search for the paint-spray shop was ultimately more successful. It necessitated a 'Dragnet' operation of mammoth proportions, for John Du Rose resolved to search every single likely building in an area parallel to the Thames, stretching from Paddington to Brentford. He also wanted to know about, as he recalls in his book, ' . . . every male in every building in this area and details of the car he owned or used. I wanted to know if he sprayed his own car, or sprayed cars for friends, or even if he owned a spray gun.' This search was to be carried out by three squads of twelve men each under a detective sergeant with each responsible for a separate sector.

Ironically the paint-spray shop was located at the furthest extremity of the search area and very near to where Bridie O'Hara's body had been found on the Heron Trading Estate. Subsequent tests proved that Bridie's body at least had been kept in a transformer building situated behind a factory and opposite a paint-spray repair shop.

It seemed clear from this discovery that the killer must have had a specialised knowledge of the huge rambling

Trading Estate that had developed haphazardly over the years and where, coincidentally, John Halliday Christie, the Rillington Place mass murderer, had worked many years before. He also must have had a legitimate reason for going there. Yet despite interviewing more than seven thousand of the people that lived on the estate, a staggering number by any standards, and keeping a twenty-four-hour watch on the comings and goings of cars entering the estate, this important breakthrough did not lead to the capture of the murderer.

John Du Rose now decided on a war of words and released a steady stream of information to the media, implying that it was just a matter of time, that the number of suspects was down to three, and that the whole of the Metropolitan Police Force had been mobilised to ensure his capture. It was hoped that this war of nerves would flush the 'Stripper' out and make him break cover. This it didn't do, for very soon it became apparent to all concerned that the killings had stopped. John Du Rose ordered an investigation on all men gaoled since the time of Bridie's body being discovered; he also checked inquest details for possible suicides covering the same period. These inquiries brought to light the apparently unremarkable suicide by gassing of a South London man. With this discovery it seemed to John Du Rose that his war of nerves had produced results after all, for, as he states in his book, 'the man I wanted to arrest took his own life; without a shadow of doubt the weight of our investigation and the inquiries that we had made about him led to the killer's committing suicide.'

What can be said about this South London man? Very little, except that he was a security guard whose hours of duty (10 pm to 6 am) would certainly have provided him with the opportunity and cover to commit the murders. He left a suicide note that was consistent enough with the case, but also typical of many such notes. It said that he was 'unable to stand the strain any longer'. His wife and family were utterly bewildered by his sudden death and could think of no good reason for it, whilst a thorough search of his house and garage turned up nothing. However, despite the apparently inconclusive evidence, John Du Rose and his team were sure that he was their man. The killings had stopped and the police search was wound down.

After such a hue and cry this closing of the 'Stripper' case was extremely unclimactic, yet curiously this is exactly what had happened in 1888 when Montague Druitt, the apparent main police suspect, committed suicide and the hunt for Jack the Ripper was called off.

There have been many theories as to the sort of man the 'Stripper' was and as to his motives. As is often the case, if the killer was the so seemingly normal South London suicide, he was clearly a person of 'Jekyll and Hyde' characteristics, capable of living an outwardly normal existence with every so often an overwhelming sexual desire compelling him to seek gratification which led to murder. The injuries to his six victims were consistent in that they all had slight bruising and scratch marks round the neck, and it would appear from this that he strangled his victims in an uncontrolled frenzy of excitement at the moment of orgasm. Indeed, it is quite possible that if only one of his victims had died in this way a manslaughter charge would have been admissible.

The two absolutely constant facts concerning the Yorkshire, Whitechapel and 'Nude' killings was that the victims were in many cases prostitutes, and that they all took place among the worst and most depressing areas contemporarily available. We have examined the almost Dantesque horror of London's late nineteenth-century East End and the sordid mean streets of Chapeltown, Manningham and Manchester's Hulme. In many respects the West London area of the early 1960s, bound by Queensway in the east, the Harrow road to the north and trailing as far to the west as Gunnersbury Park and Brentford, was similar: it was easy for the 'Stripper' to operate there and select the victims that he did.

The Royal Borough of Kensington and Chelsea has always been a divided one – this was especially true of the early 1960s, for south of the Bayswater Road and Holland Park

Avenue which acted as a sort of urban Mason-Dixon line, were the fashionable and elegant areas of W8, SW1 and SW3, which, in addition to their traditional fashionability, also at the time spawned the affluent, easy-going and trendy world of 'Swinging London' centred on the King's Road and Kensington High Street. It was a world publicised by *Time* magazine, dressed by Mary Quant and serenaded by the Beatles and the Rolling Stones.

The Borough's northern quarter was very different. Paradoxically it possessed an elegance of building that Chelsea and Kensington never had, yet it was the area of the ponce, the spiv and the get-rich-quick landlord. This was personified by Rachman, who housed as many people as he could in as few rooms as possible with as high a rent as possible. and if it wasn't paid evicted his tenants by every method, including violence, intimidation and even, on one occasion, by putting a snake in a bath. The usual victims were newly-arrived West Indians who joined the large Irish community that had always lived there and which had hitherto been the most exploited.

It is hardly surprising that these crowded and exploitative conditions produced race riots, which they did in Notting Hill, and in most respects conditions in the area were at their nadir. Attempts were made from time to time to ease conditions and the inevitable high-rise flats began to appear, particularly along the new A40 Westway motor route that was opened later. At the time the construction of this motorway did much to exacerbate the situation.

As is always the case, such a restless, depressed and volatile area, with its colourful, cosmopolitan ambience and vivid social mix (Queensway, for example, had everything from Turkish Kebab shops, Italian Spaghetti Houses, Greek delicatessens, to Whiteley's and the fashionable Queen's Skating Rink) attracted prostitutes on an unprecedented scale. For two shillings a week postcards with every kind of salacious euphemism appeared in shop windows, after night-fall a continuous stream of kerb-crawlers circled the area and dubious basement clubs with little or no regard for membership rules or licensing laws proliferated. Interestingly, the notorious 'Jazz Club' in Ledbury Road attracted so many prostitutes that a contraceptive machine was installed in the women's lavatory.

Anne Sharpley, in her marvellously evocative series of 'Murder Grove' articles that appeared during the last week of March 1965 in the London *Evening News*, noted of such a club that when one of the girls stripped to her suspenders and was passed from hand to hand her laughter was like that of an unhappy child. She also noted that the girls were depressingly resigned, frequently had 'sugar daddies', and their favourite drinks were whisky cokes.

Such observations seem to be fairly typical of the thousands of prostitutes that flocked in from the provinces, frequently starting on the 'game' by working for a ponce, 'because they had been kind' – their particular trademark a tattoo testifying to this by referring to him by name – and over the years becoming hardened, embittered and fatalistic. Very often they never had actual sexual intercourse with their clients but indulged in (often violent) deviational acts with them. Ann Sharpley again noted this typical reaction to a girl's clients : 'Revolting dirty old bastards. I hate them . . . they can't get satisfaction from their wives and they are not man enough to tell them they have a kink so they come to a prostitute.'

It is interesting to note that Helen Barthelemy was warned by the police shortly before her murder. We have seen how a young girl was soliciting in Huddersfield's Great Northern Street only a few hours after the discovery of Helen Rytka's murder. Yet such fatalism is not so surprising if one considers the following observation, again from Anne Sharpley : 'Whores have a sort of strange courage that enables them day after day to meet clients, any of whom may be a murderer, and indeed they deal in so much simulated and actual violence, what is death but the next step? No wonder they are not afraid.'

It would seem in this case, as with the Whitechapel murders and the Yorkshire Ripper, that prostitutes were obviously sought since they would be willing, unsuspicious, often drunk or under the influence of drugs, and fatalistically disposed towards violence. Of equal importance, well summed up in G. K. Chesterton's observation : 'Where is the best place to hide a leaf? In a tree,' is the fact that if a murderer were to have any chance of getting away with it he would have to do what a lot of other people were doing too, and in Chapeltown, Notting Hill and Whitechapel a lot of people were picking up prostitutes.

It is true that a letter that possibly, though by no means certainly, came from Jack the Ripper, stated, ' . . . I am down on Whores', and that the Yorkshire Ripper in his alleged tape to George Oldfield said, 'There's plenty of them knocking about . . . they never learn, do they, George? I bet you've warned them but they never listen.' However, the Yorkshire Ripper's comment seems to express surprise at the ease with which he picks up his victims rather than any dislike of them. It is also extremely significant in this respect that at least three of the murdered women had not been prostitutes at all. Indeed, given the opportunity, there seems very little reason to suppose that any subsequent victim would necessarily be a prostitute either.

We have already established that one advantage of selecting prostitutes as victims is the smoke-screen that surrounds a police investigation of this nature with invariably a great reluctance for witnesses to come forward. This can only help the killer.

Kenneth Archibald's confession demonstrates how apparently seriously the police initially took this confession, because of the accuracy with which Irene Lockwood's clothes and accent were described, and because of the previous 'Kenny is coming' diary entry. Clearly Archibald, having read the press reports, made intelligent guesses which seemed to fit. All this shows how relatively easy it is to hit upon facts that could appear to be significant to the police but in reality are only lucky guesses. Detectives handling the Whitechapel case experienced this with the letter and postcard, dated 25th September 1888 and 30th September

1888 respectively, that were sent to the Central News Agency and signed Jack the Ripper. The fact that they referred to two things that were thought only the killer could know made them appear genuine. However, later the then head of the CID, Sir Melville MacNaughten, wrote in his memoirs: 'In this ghastly production I have always thought I could discern the stained forefinger of the journalist – indeed a year later I had shrewd suspicions as to the actual author!' I mention those examples solely to illustrate how difficult it is for the police, whether in verbal, written or taped form, to separate the wood from the trees and to illustrate how easy it is to be misled by apparent corroborating evidence.

We do not know to what extent the police have been plagued with false confessions on this occasion. However, one case has already come to Court. This involved an alcoholic who set fire to somebody's room. Apparently in an effort to deflect police attention he confessed to the Ripper killings. The man received a suitably stiff sentence.

In his study *Sexual Perversion and Abnormalities*, Dr Clifford Allen makes the point that confessions, bogus or otherwise, should invariably be taken seriously. He quotes cases where confessions have been dismissed and the man sent away only to commit a murder within a matter of hours or a few days. Ideally, everyone making a confession should be held and thoroughly investigated.

It is a fair bet that Jack the Ripper committed suicide. The police are convinced that Jack the Stripper did the same. There would appear to be a strong possibility that the Yorkshire killer will do likewise. Indeed he has threatened to do so (if the tape is genuine). It is conceivable we will never know; but unless the police are able to tie up a suicide with firm forensic evidence it is bound to be a long time yet before they can state definitely that the current spate of murders is at an end.

CHAPTER THIRTEEN

Conclusion

In July 1979 *The Guardian* reported that by that stage in the inquiry about 500 officers were involved in the Ripper case, and over 250,000 man-hours had already been spent, at a cost exceeding £3 million. All kinds of other statistics have been given, all of which have been rendered out of date by the continuing heavy police commitment to the investigation. By mid-summer 1979 over 20,000 statements had been gathered and more than 150,000 leads had been examined. Not less than 137,000 vehicles had been checked.

The full extent of the police commitment is revealed in Mr Ronald Gregory's annual report as Chief Constable of the West Yorkshire Police. In June 1979 Mr Gregory reported that 259 officers, including 120 detectives (of the West Yorkshire Force) were engaged full time on the Ripper case. This obviously imposed a considerable strain on the county police force which was in any case nearly 500 officers below establishment level. The Chief Constable said in his report that the Ripper investigation was proving to be one of the most protracted murder inquiries in the history of the police service.

The long-term detachment of almost a quarter of the detective strength to the Ripper inquiry had imposed a crippling burden on manpower and finance. In a county where 123,166 crimes had been recorded in the previous twelve months (an average of fourteen every hour) the strain on resources was obviously keenly felt. However, Mr Gregory was able to draw satisfaction from the fact that the general detection rate remained above the national average.

The Ripper investigation must have also imposed some

strain on the resources of the Greater Manchester Force and the Lancashire and Northumbrian police, though this is obviously not so keenly felt as in West Yorkshire, which has borne the brunt of the inquiry. In fact the real costs of the inquiry may well be greater than the published estimates, because a variety of below-the-line costs are obviously not included.

This was brought home to me forcibly both in Bradford and Preston where I was lengthily interviewed by pairs of CID officers about my own inquiries. These officers were not involved in any specific Ripper assignment. The fact is that the sheer size of the manhunt for Britain's No. 1 fugitive has so impressed the ordinary policeman that he is desperately keen to get his share of the action.

Assuming that an arrest is not long delayed, I would estimate that the total cost of the Ripper hunt will climb to upwards of £4 million. I would further estimate that the interval between arrest and trial will prove to be somewhat protracted and expensive requiring a great deal of further investigation and liaison between police forces. Quite naturally, the various police forces involved will be anxious to clear up their own Ripper murders and to secure convictions where possible.

The kind of totally inhuman pattern of random murder which this book sets out to examine is the most difficult to solve. The killer may appear to his workmates completely normal. Even members of his own family may have no suspicion of his double life. The police are looking for a needle in a haystack. It is mainly because of the murderer's own flamboyance and desire for self-publicity that a profile of the killer is beginning to emerge. Paradoxically in private life the murderer may seem both quiet and withdrawn.

The murderer has now claimed more than twice the number of victims killed by Jack the Ripper, who did all his killing between August and November 1888. He has killed many more than the Moors Murderers, Graham Young the poisoner, or the Black Panther.

Jack the Ripper, and the London Nude murderer, who killed six times in the middle sixties, were never caught. On the other hand, George Cummins, who killed four times during the war, and Christie, who killed seven times, were both found and convicted.

The current North of England killings seem to be completely random or spasmodic in nature, and cannot reasonably be linked with any causative factor. It has been established that there is no link with the phases of the moon; nor is there any climatic or seasonal link. Again, although the murder dates are not precise in every case, they do seem to occur on almost any day of the week. No discernible pattern seems to emerge. The first two vicious assaults, where both victims survived, occurred within about one month of each other in July and August, 1975. There then appears to have been a pause until 29th October of the same year when Wilma McCann was murdered. A further murder occurred a month later, and one the following January. There then occurred a long interval of fifty-four weeks from 21st January 1976 until 6th February 1977. In 1977, however, the killer struck six times, two of his victims surviving, Maureen Long and Marilyn Moore. In 1978 the Ripper killed twice in January, at Huddersfield and Bradford, and again in May at Manchester. His last murder to date was that of Barbara Leach in Bradford in September 1979.

One of the most puzzling features of the Ripper inquiry is the long intervals which have occurred between killings; in particular between the murder of Emily Jackson in January 1976 and that of Irene Richardson in February 1977. There was again a gap of nearly a year between the murder of Vera Millward in May 1978 and that of Josephine Whitaker in April 1979. During these two intervals it is thought there were no other Ripper attacks on women of a non-fatal character, the killer, it would seem, remained completely quiescent. This remains a mystery to both psychiatrists and policemen. It has been assumed by the authorities, from an early stage in the inquiry, that the psychological reasons underlying the killer's attacks would of their very nature precipitate further murders. If I am correct in placing the Ripper in the category of Violent Sex Offender, as defined by Don Gibbons, I would anticipate, if anything, an intensification of savage acts. The career of the London Nude Murderer produced a killing on average about every two months. In the case of Jack the Ripper five killings occurred between the end of August and early November of the same year, with if anything mounting ferocity. The most plausible assumption in both cases is that the impulse to kill was only extinguished by suicide. Other killers like Kurten, Petiot and probably Heath, whom we have examined in this volume, demonstrate an increasing potential to kill, this being finally frustrated by the arrest of the killer. In other cases mentioned the killer has curtailed his own murderous instincts by making a confession to the police.

In this context the Ripper remains an enigma; so much so that Dr Stephen Shaw was at one stage induced to speculate that the Ripper may have taken a wife. This is an obvious possibility, but in view of the case histories we have examined this would not necessarily produce an end to the spate of murders. Certain psychiatric opinion suggests that the psychopath may eventually outgrow violent and brutal anti-social behaviour as he finally adjusts to society in middle age. This theory has, however, been upset by the resumption of further acts of atrocity.

The police have, of course, examined the possibility that the Ripper was in prison for other offences between outrages. With a continually changing male prison population of about 40,000, tracing is obviously difficult, but police have been assisted by the tape-recording which has been played in gaols up and down the country in the hope that prison officers may be able to identify the voice of the killer. Again, there is the possibility that the Ripper could have been admitted to a secure mental asylum to receive treatment for a psychopathic disorder. So far diligent research in this area has failed to turn anything up.

One theory which has not been mentioned so far is that

the killer could be a seaman, possibly engaged in coastal navigation, who from time to time undertakes longer journeys. This theory may account for the irregular frequency of the killings, and could also account for the Ripper's 'manual' and 'engineering' skills. It might also enable him to dispose of soiled clothing. This theory would presuppose that he has facilities for garaging a car. When questioned on this theory a Ripper Squad detective said, 'It just cannot be ruled out that the man we are seeking has some sort of connection with seafaring.'

Another theory is that he is a long-distance lorry driver. Police examined this possibility after the murder of Joan Harrison in Preston. A lorry would be ideal for hiding soiled clothing and also the murder weapons, which could form part of a tool kit. Also a long-distance lorry driver may well have a familiarity with a number of northern towns, but would not necessarily live in any of the towns involved. Neilson, the Black Panther, for example, lived in Bradford but did his killing in the Midlands. In any transport café where customers would be expected to have a variety of regional accents his voice would be unlikely to give him away. He could in addition spend long periods sleeping in the cab. Again in this instance he would have to have garage parking facilities for his motor car.

If I may be allowed to set out a personal theory at this stage it is that the Ripper may well be a member of a uniformed profession. The association between the concept of uniform and several of the cases we have examined does suggest that this avenue of inquiry might prove profitable. A uniform can provide a certain anonymity, as has been shown in the London Nude murder case, where the killer conducted the slaughter during working hours as a security man. Other areas of employment which might prove attractive to the psychopath include the fire service, the police force and the armed services. It would come as no surprise to discover that the Ripper had sought a career in any of these. The authorities are of course alert to the dangers of recruiting unbalanced psychopathic types. However, conflict arises from the fact that the qualities looked for in the recruit do coincide with certain aspects of the psychopathic personality. The possibility, for example, that the Ripper has at some time been recruited into the army as an NCO and subsequently cashiered, possibly after serving a term of glass-house imprisonment, cannot be dismissed.

By his actions, the Ripper suggests to me a certain tactical expertise, a background of military training and a disciplined approach. It has been noted that the Ripper demonstrates a cool cunning and intelligence, and lack of nervousness. He would appear to be both brutal and disciplined in the sense that he does not leave behind an abundance of clues at the scene of the crime. His ability to melt into the darkness almost suggests guerrilla training. Again, his obvious strength and agility suggest to me training in certain athletic skills, which, like the Black Panther, he may have kept up after his departure from the service. The long intervals between murders could possibly be explained by service tours overseas in Northern Ireland, Germany or Hong Kong and even Home postings under strict military supervision. The fact that the Ripper could have a car garaged at home whilst serving in the regular army would not appear strange. Also if, as is thought, the Ripper exhibits evidence of a grounding in a craft skill, this too could be acquired in the regular army.

Doubtless it is unwise to speculate, but in the present state of knowledge and in the light of the huge police commitment to the case, it might just pay someone to nose about in the Ministry of Defence, checking regimental movements to discover whether absences abroad coincide with the interruptions in the Ripper's activities. It would probably be best to start with regiments which draw a significant proportion of their recruits from the region where it is felt the Ripper originates. The First Battalion Royal Regiment of Fusiliers, the King's Own Border Regiment and the Scottish Borderers are given merely as examples of where to start to look. Regimental medical departments will doubtless be prepared to discuss the dossiers of a few 'suspect' cases with the appropriate authorities.

On 15th May 1979 the *Yorkshire Evening Post* published a graphic Special Report by its Chief Crime Reporter, Bruce Smith. The full page feature included a large blank square containing a question mark, entitled 'Face of the Ripper?' Alongside this was an appeal to *Evening Post* readers to cast their minds back more than three years and answer the following questions.

I would like, in conclusion, to list these questions which the police obviously consider practical and direct and which may point the way to the killer.

Ask Yourself These Questions:

1 Do you know a man who works in an engineering-type trade who visited the North East, including Sunderland, on 7th or 8th March and 12th or 13th March 1978, and 22nd and 23rd March this year? (These dates obviously refer to the dates of letters posted to George Oldfield and the *Daily Mirror*.)

2 Do you know of a man who visited people, perhaps friends or relatives, in that region on those dates?

3 Do you know of a man who has talked of visiting many of the 'murder towns' around the relevant dates?

4 Is this person connected with engineering? If not, has he had any connection with engineering?
   THE NEXT QUESTIONS, HOWEVER DISLOYAL THEY MAY SEEM, MUST BE ANSWERED IF THE COUNTRY IS TO BE FREED FROM THE THREAT OF THE RIPPER.

5 Do you have a husband, father, brother, son, fiancé, boyfriend or neighbour with access to a car whose whereabouts on the murder nights are not known or cannot be established?

6 If so, has this person any history of employment in the engineering industry?

7 Do you know of any large quantity of clothing this man may have disposed of?

8   Is he in the habit of returning home or leaving unusually late or in the early hours?

9   Does he visit the North East, have friends or relatives there, or has he worked there in the last thirteen months?

Both the Chief Constable of West Yorkshire, Mr Ronald Gregory and George Oldfield have expressed a wish to hear from the Ripper, and to hear some of his motives for the gruesome killings. What I, and I'm sure millions of others, want answered is, what compels a man to undertake such a 'journey through the inferno of human brutalities'.

Finally, I will add a few further suggestions of my own. I would suggest that the Ripper probably began his murderous career in his late twenties and I would think it not unlikely that he is now in his early to mid-thirties – let us say thirty-two. This indicates a date of birth shortly after the war. Basing my assessment on a study of case histories, an unhappy family background would seem to be indicated. The presence of a violent and drunken father, an incestuous relationship with a mother or sister, are the kind of factors which provide a formative influence in the development of a sadistic psychopath. By the late fifties we are looking for a boy of about twelve, quiet, withdrawn, probably already noted for sadistic treatment of animals, thieving, possibly fire-raising and general anti-social behaviour. By this time the child may well be in local authority care, where he may have become noted for a bullying tendency, though probably generally quiet and subordinate. By sixteen he will probably have been judged intelligent enough to pursue a technical course. This could, as already suggested, have been followed by admission into the armed forces for a three-year term or perhaps longer. It is unlikely, by this stage, that even close contemporaries would have noticed anything particularly abnormal. It is just possible, however, that people, now in their early thirties, may with prompting recall something strange about the adolescent's feelings towards women. This might have taken the form of unnatural restraint, expressions of hatred or a sudden unrestrained response accompanied by the infliction of pain or the partial throttling of a girl. The kind of thing that can happen at a party when things get out of hand and where everyone has had too much to drink, leaving no more than a distasteful memory lingering in the subconscious. Girls rarely report these minor attacks to the police.

Writing this volume prior to the arrest of the killer has led to much speculation on the part of the author. It is my firm hope, but not my expectation, that the killer will have been apprehended before this is published. If he has not been brought to book I hope that some of the ideas contained here may provoke a thought or a recollection which will lead to the murderer.

Chronology of Murdered Women

1 WILMA McCANN   29th October 1975   LEEDS
   Found Prince Philip
   playing fields,
   Scott Hall Avenue,
   Chapelton, Leeds

2 JOAN HARRISON   20th November 1975 PRESTON
   Found in garage
   in Preston

3 EMILY JACKSON   21st January 1976   LEEDS
   Found in a cul-de-sac
   near Sheepscarp,
   North St junction, Leeds

4 IRENE RICHARDSON   6th February 1977   LEEDS
   Found Soldiers Field,
   Roundhay Park, Leeds

5 PATRICIA ATKINSON   24th April 1977   BRADFORD
   Found in her own bed,
   Oak Avenue, Manningham,
   Bradford

6 JAYNE MacDONALD   25th June 1977   LEEDS
   Found near Chapeltown
   Community Centre, Leeds

7 JEAN ROYLE or JORDAN   10th October 1977   MANCHESTER
   Found on allotments,
   Chorlton-cum-Hardy,
   Manchester

8 HELEN or ELENA RYTKA 31st January 1978   HUDDERSFIELD
  Found in timberyard,
  Great Northern Street,
  Huddersfield

9 YVONNE PEARSON   21st January 1978   BRADFORD
  Found on 26th March,
  wasteland, Whetley Hill,
  Bradford

10 VERA MILLWARD   16th May 1978   MANCHESTER
  Found in the grounds of
  Manchester Royal
  Infirmary

11 JOSEPHINE WHITAKER   4th April 1979   HALIFAX
  Found in Savile Park,
  Halifax

12 BARBARA LEACH   2nd September 1979 BRADFORD
  Found at
  Back Ashgrove,
  Bradford

Chronology of Injured Women

1 ANNA ROGULSKI   5th July 1975   KEIGHLEY
  Alice Street,
  Keighley

2 OLIVE SMELT   15th August 1975   HALIFAX
  Woodside Mount,
  Halifax

3 MAUREEN LONG   10th July 1977   BRADFORD
  Waste ground,
  Bowling Back Lane,
  Bradford

4 MARILYN MOORE   14th December 1977 LEEDS
  Lay-by, Buslingthorpe
  Lane, Leeds

Bibliography

1   *A Calendar of Murder*, Terence Morris and Louis Blom-Cooper, Michael Joseph, 1964.

2   *The Sadist*, Karl Berg.

3   *The Complete Jack the Ripper*, Donald Rumbelow, W. H. Allen and Co. Ltd, 1975.

4   *Murder Investigation*, Frederick Oughton, Elek Books Ltd, 1971.

5   *Inner City Crisis, Manchester's Hulme*, Peter Thomson, published by Hulme People's Rights Centre, Manchester.

6   *The Detection of Secret Homicide*, J. D. J. Havard, MA, LLB, MB BCher, Macmillan and Co. Ltd, 1960.

7   *Society Crime and Criminal Careers*, D. C. Gibbons, Prentice Hall, 1968.

8   *The Death Doctors*, Arthur Kent, New English Library 1974.

9   *Murder was my Business*, John Du Rose, W. H. Allen and Co. Ltd, 1973.

10 *Jack the Ripper*, Dan Farson, Michael Joseph, 1972.

11 *Sexual Perversion and Abnormalities*, Clifford Allen, Oxford Medical Publication OUP, 1949.

12 *The Mask of Sanity*, Hervey Cleckley, C. V. Mosby Co., 1964.

13 *Personality Types Among Abnormal Homicides*, R. Blackburn, British Journal of Criminology.

14 *Aberrations of the Sexual Life: The Psychopathia Sexualis*, R. V. Krafft-Ebing, Staples Press Ltd, 1959.

15 *Handbook of Abnormal Psychology*, (ed.) H. J. Eysenck, Pitman Medical, 1973.

16 *Psychopathy and Delinquency*, W. & J. McCord, Grune and Stratton, 1956.

17 *Criminology*, M. Haskel and L. Yablonsky, Rand McNally, 1978.

18 *Personality Types Among Abnormal Homicides*, R. Blackburn, British Journal of Criminology, 1971.

19 *H.M.S.O. Murder 1957–1968*, Home Office Research Studies, No. 3, 1969.

Wyndham Books are obtainable from many booksellers and newsagents. If you have any difficulty please send purchase price plus postage on the scale below to:

Wyndham Cash Sales,
P.O. Box 11,
Falmouth,
Cornwall

OR

Star Book Service,
G.P.O. Box 29,
Douglas,
Isle of Man,
British Isles

While every effort is made to keep prices low, it is sometimes necessary to increase prices at short notice. Wyndham Books reserve the right to show new retail prices on covers which may differ from those advertised in the text or elsewhere.

Postage and Packing Rate
U.K.
One book 25p plus 10p per copy for each additional book ordered to a maximum charge of £1.05

B.F.P.O. and Eire
One book 25p plus 10p per copy for the next 8 books and thereafter 5p per book. Overseas 40p for the first book and 12p per copy for each additional book.